Card of the Day
TAROT

Quick and Easy One-Card Tarot Readings for
Love, Work, and Everyday Life

---×---

KERRY WARD
illustrations by Adam Oehlers

Quarto.com

© 2024 Quarto Publishing Group USA Inc.
Text © 2024 Kerry Ward
Illustrations © 2024 A. R. Oehlers

First Published in 2024 by Fair Winds Press, an imprint of The Quarto Group,
100 Cummings Center, Suite 265-D, Beverly, MA 01915, USA.
T (978) 282-9590 F (978) 283-2742

Fair Winds Press titles are also available at discount for retail, wholesale, promotional,
and bulk purchase. For details, contact the Special Sales Manager by email at
specialsales@quarto.com or by mail at The Quarto Group, Attn: Special Sales Manager,
100 Cummings Center, Suite 265-D, Beverly, MA 01915, USA.

28 27 26 25 24   1 2 3 4 5

ISBN: 978-0-7603-8563-0

Digital edition published in 2024
eISBN: 978-0-7603-8564-7

Library of Congress Cataloging-in-Publication Data

Names: Ward, Kerry Louise, author.
Title: Card of the day tarot : quick and easy one-card tarot readings for
   love, work, and everyday life / Kerry Ward.
Description: Beverly, MA : Fair Winds Press, 2024. | Includes index. |
   Summary: "Featuring 12 unique tarot rituals, Card of the Day Tarot is
   the ultimate guide to performing practical and insightful one-card tarot
   readings in your everyday life"-- Provided by publisher.
Identifiers: LCCN 2023025771 | ISBN 9780760385630 | ISBN 9780760385647
   (ebook)
Subjects: LCSH: Tarot.
Classification: LCC BF1879.T2 W349 2024 | DDC 133.3/2424--dc23/eng/20230606
LC record available at https://lccn.loc.gov/2023025771

Illustration: Adam Oehlers

Printed in China

This book is dedicated to all the dusty tarot decks out there, patiently waiting for their owners' time and attention. It's coming soon, I promise. This book will change everything. Get ready to be used, appreciated, and admired every day!

CONTENTS

Introduction

I have been immersed in the tarot world for more than twenty-five years, and I know the pitfalls. I know where and when people run out of steam, stop trying, and put their deck back on the shelf, where it gathers dust and becomes a thing they "were into once."

Shall I tell you what the biggest pitfall is?

It's creating spreads—using multiple questions and cards in one reading. Spreads get complicated, confusing, and challenging. You are trying to find a thread, a consistent theme, a singular answer, but with all these random cards with different suits, numbers, people, and messages in the mix, it can be incredibly messy and frustrating. Not to mention time-consuming!

So I have written this book. It will work with any tarot deck (though not oracle cards; that is a different kettle of fish). I provide simple, comprehensive meanings for every card so that instead of doing lengthy multi-card readings, you can get everything you need from a simple one-card pull. No more spreads. Whatever you want to know, one card will do it.

Really?! Yes.

Tapping into tarot's natural flexibility, I have rewritten the card descriptions to answer pretty much any question. I have also created a series of suggested one-card rituals and ideas to get you started. From questions about love and work, to connecting with passed loves ones, to getting your day started in the right way, tarot can be there for you 24/7, 365 days a year!

One-card tarot readings are one of the easiest, fastest, and best ways to bring the wisdom of the tarot into your daily life. These readings are also the best way to get to know your tarot cards, activate your intuition, and enjoy your tarot deck. Because you are zooming in on one picture, you can really take the time to assess what the single card prompts in your mind, memory, and body. You can think about one card at a deeper level for a longer time rather than splitting your attention across many cards.

Plus, one-card readings are fast. There's no need to set aside a good half an hour or longer to dwell on your cards, their interlinking elements, their subtle asides, and their overall story . . . it's just one card. Easy!

It's no wonder "card of the day" style readings are so popular. Whether you are a beginner or an experienced reader, a single card truly can make all the difference. I hope this book reactivates your appetite for the cards, hones your understanding of their messages, and helps you find your path toward doing useful, real-life tarot card readings in your everyday life.

Using Tarot for One-Card Draws

The following one-card tarot rituals provide you with inspiration for simple ways of using your tarot deck throughout the day to inform, inspire, and impact your everyday life.

I will take you through twelve different one-card pulls, some of which include a little bit of ritualistic practice to make the experience more of an event—to evoke enchantment and to make the daily grind feel a little more magical and full of possibility. Tarot can do this for you. It can bring magic to the humdrum.

On the other side of the spectrum, some of the one-card pulls are purely practical and functional, designed to answer specific queries relating to popular themes (e.g., career, love) or to answer simple yes/no questions.

You are welcome to use any of these pulls, if you find them useful, in your daily life, but know that they are merely suggestions: a card-of-the-day starter pack! You can—and should—notice the moments in your own daily life when you feel in need of a bit of extra direction, new inputs, or guidance. When those moments appear, draw out your deck and pull a card.

Create your own rituals. Fulfill your own needs.

12

Card-of-the-Day

TAROT

RITUALS

✕

① Good Morning! Tarot

This little ritual could become a habitual way for you to start each day. Or you could save it for those days when you know you might wake up feeling a little sluggish, reluctant, or even nervous to embark upon what lies ahead.

The trick here is to set it all up the night before so that you awaken with a sense of excitement and fall into the ritual first thing.

Next to or near your bedside, arrange your tarot cards, a tall glass of water (maybe with a slice of lemon), and either a candle or a vial or spritzer of essential oil or fragrance. Citrus, herbal, eucalyptus, and mint scents are good for waking your senses up in a positive way. If there is a Full or New Moon, consider placing these items on your windowsill for an extra dose of lunar magic.

To make your ritual even more special, replace the glass of water with a pre-prepared elixir. Savor the ritual of selecting your best cup or glass and pouring your chosen liquid (along with any fruits, herbs, cordials, etc.) into it. As you pour, state an intention aloud. For example, you could say something like "I will drink this to awaken my best self." Place your hands over the cup and visualize a bright light entering the drink, symbolizing the power of your intention. Focus on the purpose of your intention as you imagine that light growing stronger until it beams from the vessel out into the room. When you drink the elixir the next morning, imagine this powerful white light swirling around the liquid as it enters your body and brings the intention home to you.

When you wake up, without getting up if possible, open your window slightly, light your candle, and spritz your essential oil. Drink your water or elixir to cleanse your system after a long sleep. Consider putting on an ambience video related to the current season or weather or listen to the radio, classical music, or even just the white noise from outside. Stretch your body, wiggle your feet and hands, and roll your neck gently. You might wish to do some bed-friendly yoga stretches if you enjoy that practice. Run your attention over your body and notice any part that feels sore, stiff, or in need of extra attention. Visualize that area softening, glowing, and relaxing.

Mentally scan your day ahead and acknowledge the tasks ahead of you. Don't think about how you will do them; just acknowledge they are on the list. Ask yourself, "What am I excited about? What am I nervous about? What am I irritated about?" Acknowledge your emotions and their drivers. Say aloud a short, direct affirmation that you feel will give you the power or energy you need to make this day a great one, for example, "I can handle it" or "I will meet these challenges with composure and capability."

Still in bed, but now more awake and engaged with the day ahead, start to shuffle your cards. You can ask yourself a specific question pertaining to your day's schedule and events, or you can ask a question such as one of the following:

What will be the biggest opportunity to fulfill my potential today?
What guiding light and wisdom will steer me through today?
What am I going to be most excited about today?
What single step can I take to positively challenge myself and grow today?
How can I make my corner of the Earth a better place today?

Pull your card and read its interpretation. Focus on the things that resonate with, inspire, or reach you most deeply or most positively. Note them in your journal or on your phone. You can even take a picture of the card to work as a prompt throughout the day ahead. This card sets the tone for your day, giving you an underlying purpose of or meaning to the events about to unfold. It gives you an anchor and a grounding force to make sense of whatever happens, and it helps you glide through your day, find wisdom, and enjoy your experiences.

② Game Face Tarot

The rituals you already undertake to get washed, dressed, accessorized, fragranced, and maybe made up for the day ahead already have their own structure and pace. Tarot can easily be incorporated to make a tangible impact on your mood and outlook, and it can help you put on your chosen game face for the day (or night).

Before you start getting ready, sit down at your dressing table, vanity, or bathroom mirror with your cards in hand. Ask yourself what you wish to bring to the day ahead, what you're presenting to the wider world, and how you want to interact and make an impact.

Shuffle the deck and pull a card. Prop it up on your mirror or place where you can see it. Read your card's interpretation, consider its messages, and focus on the one that resonates most with you right now. Make a note of the associated affirmation. You can now use your card to make some conscious choices about your physical preparation for today.

Consider how you will use fragrance in bathing, body care, and perfume. Is today a fun, outgoing, social day? That might call for something light, fruity, and floral. Or is it more of an intense, focused, get-stuff-done day that would be better suited to something citrusy, sharp, or herbal? Are you looking to stoke your inner power, charisma, or attractiveness? Then maybe you should go with something that has earthy, woody, musky notes. Consider the card you pulled and the fragrances available to you. What are you drawn toward?

Next, think about your outfit and accessories. Much has been said recently about dopamine dressing, which is largely based on color therapy. This approach is based on the idea that how we look directly affects our mood and confidence. Dressing to feel good is not only about wearing things that suit you or feel comfortable and pleasing; it is also about using color and texture to comfort you, relax you, enliven you, and boost your energy. We all carry psychological connections to different colors stemming from childhood. The same is even true of textures—for instance, wool provokes a very different sensation and a very different emotion than satin or silk does. When considering color in dressing, here are some basic guidelines:

Red enlivens, empowers, and energizes.
Yellow amplifies hope, optimism, and luck.
Blue soothes, heals, and promotes peace.

Green is relaxing, is easing, and invokes a connection to your creativity.
Orange is a positivity-, social-, and good times–booster.
Purple links to our psychic skills, inner wisdom, and intuition.

Does your card directly associate with any of these feelings or states of mind? And can you wear that color or accessorize an outfit with that color to help you remember your card's positive message today? Maybe your jewelry could provide the right colors and prompts.

Finally, getting ready and facing a mirror is a great window of time for saying affirmations. Every card in the deck has an affirmation linked to it, so you can use your card's affirmation at this time. Studies prove that positive affirmations help activate parts of the brain that are associated with self-related processing and reward. The same studies also indicate that positive affirmations can help build or restore self-confidence.

Affirmations work on three levels. The first (and most superficial) is thought: You will think the words literally. The second, getting more real now, is emotion. You can experience or stimulate the feelings associated with those words. Even faking the associated emotions can create the same benefits, as the mind often cannot distinguish between real and perceived. The final level, and the part where change occurs, is belief: truly believing what you are saying and knowing, deep down, that it applies to you and that you can do what you set out to do. Say your affirmations three times out loud, and let each recital permeate to the next level until you truly believe what you are saying. Repeat your affirmations during the day and again at night. After thirty days of sustained affirmations, you should notice your self-talk becoming more positive and encouraging by default, versus having to force it.

You may wish to keep your card with you throughout the day or to take a picture of it or leave it on your mirror to reflect on later, when you get home or complete your tasks.

❸ Tarot on the Go

It's a fact of life that we all have ups and downs throughout the day. On any given day, you might experience fatigue, boredom, apathy, or stress. Negative emotions can threaten to settle in and derail your good intentions and positive progress. But here's a secret: You can use your tarot deck as a means of recalibrating and rebooting your mood during the day. Keep your deck with you and, when a downer strikes, take it out and pull yourself a mood-refreshing card!

First, settle yourself and perform a super-quick on-the-go mood exercise to ensure you're already halfway back to feeling great again. You can choose from one of the following rituals, depending on how you're feeling or what you need, or you can do your own thing—whatever gets you in the right headspace.

Mood Exercise 1: Grounding Power

Use this technique when you feel tired, low, unstable, or like you need to ground and balance your energy.

1. Close your eyes and take three deep breaths.

2. Visualize a light at the core of your body (that might be your stomach, heart, solar plexus, or wherever you feel your core is centered).

3. Visualize a tendril of this light growing down from your core toward the ground. See it penetrate the floor, deep down into the earth's core.

4. Draw some of the earth's core energy up through your tendril, like a straw.

5. Let the earth's energy fill your body.

Mood Exercise 2: Sunbathing Booster

Tap into the magical energy of the sun to help lift your spirits! Get outside if you can or sit next to an open window.

1. Sit in a comfortable spot where you can feel the sunlight on your body.

2. Close your eyes and imagine a fine, green mist rising from the ground and all the living, growing things around you.

3. Take three slow, deep breaths. Each time you inhale, visualize that mist of vibrant green energy flowing into your lungs and spreading through your body.

4. As you exhale, release tension and stress.

5. Open your awareness to the warmth of the sunlight. Receive it fully.

6. Let it in and notice what energy it brings to you.

How do you feel physically, emotionally, and spiritually? What messages, thoughts, or ideas are you being gifted? What sensations flow through you? What feelings arise?

Take as long as you wish to commune with the sun's energy. When you are finished, take a final three deep breaths and open your eyes.

Mood Exercise 3: Psychic Protection Shield

This quick exercise is for times when someone else has rattled you and you need to protect yourself.

1. Take several slow, deep, calming breaths. You are safe.

2. Envision the outer layers of your aura becoming reflective so that anything impinging on it is deflected, like light from a mirror. This shield makes it hard for others to sense and read you.

3. Experiment with visualizing different types of mirrored surface: metallic, ceramic, white, silver, dark, glossy, matte, and so on. When you've visualized, and therefore activated, your shield, return to the fray confident in the knowledge that you're now protected from damaging auras and energies around you.

Ask Your Question

Once you've completed your mood ritual and you feel grounded, energized, and secure, pull out your cards and ask your question. It could be any of the following examples or one of your own design specifically related to what you've experienced that day. Be specific when forming a question.

Why do I feel down?
What kind of person do I want to be for the rest of today?
What can I learn from my mistake(s) today?
What should my priority be for the rest of today?
What is my guiding light for the rest of today?
Whom should I gravitate toward and make an effort to talk to today?
What can I look forward to later on?
What could the life lesson of today be?
What do I need to know now?
What should I be grateful for today?
What is my immediate next step after this reading?

Pull your card and read its interpretation. Focus on the things that resonate, inspire, or touch a nerve. Mentally note them, or even take a picture of the card to work with it as a prompt. Think, now, about how you can use the message from the card to influence the next hour of your day. What immediate and overt course of action can you take to make a positive difference by using that card?

Now, get back to it!

4 Yes or No Tarot

Most people assume tarot is best for answering deep, complicated questions with multiple layers and serious ramifications. But your tarot deck can just as easily provide quick (in fact, instant) answers to simple yes-or-no questions, anytime and anyplace. And you only need to pull a single card.

The methodology is simple. Some cards mean yes; some cards mean no. These assignments will differ from person to person. For the purposes of this book, I have assigned a yes or a no to each card in its description. You can use that as a starting point. Consider also using the rest of the card's information to further inform your decision, probe your intentions, and suggest further questions to ask or reflections to consider.

First, you must think of your yes/no question. It should be specific and direct. Resist the impulse to weave more questions in because you won't know which part of the question is being answered when you get your yes or no. If you sense yourself doing this, pull your questions apart and ask each of them separately. It helps to jot them down. So, for example, instead of "Does X want to carry on this relationship because they love me?" try "Does X love me?" and then "Does X want to carry on this relationship?"

When you have your question in mind clearly, shuffle the deck and pull a card. Head to the bottom of that card's interpretation in this book to find your answer.

The yes/no answers in this book are the personal interpretations of one reader (me) based on experience with the cards and the cards' overall positive or negative energy. In truth, none of the tarot cards can offer a 100 percent firm yes-or-no answer. They are much more expansive than that, and they live in shades of gray. If the interpretations in this book don't feel right to you, feel free to recalibrate them. You can decide in advance which cards mean yes and which mean no. Maybe all Coins and Cups mean yes and all Swords and Wands mean no, for example. You might even choose to use just ten or twenty cards for this practice, shuffling them first, to keep it simple.

A good way to sense if the answer feels right to you is to check in with your body. What is your immediate gut reaction to the answer? What sensations are you physically experiencing and where? If your body feels open, relaxed, and maybe even tingly or energized, then you are ready to lean into your decision and make it happen. If you experience any tensing, tightening, closing, shrinking, or stiffening, then something is making you uneasy, anxious, or unsure.

Spend a little time talking to that feeling (inside your mind). Zoom in on the sensation and try to imagine what it might look, sound, smell, and feel like. Give it a personality or shape. If you were to ask this feeling what it wanted to tell you, what would it say? Your body holds a great deal more intelligence and wisdom than it's given credit for. Most information hits and resonates within our body before it reaches our mind, so take a moment and just listen.

If you still feel unsure or undecided, sleep on it. Go to bed imagining you had taken the recommended course of action and notice how easily, quickly, and deeply you experience sleep that night. Are your thoughts troubled or free? A good night's sleep reinforces that you are making the right choice. A poor night's sleep requires more consideration. You might spend the following night imagining you had taken the alternative course of action. Compare and contrast your responses to each scenario.

Ultimately, you can only make a choice based on what you know, feel, and believe in that moment. Nothing is guaranteed, foolproof, or certain. Do your best, keep moving, and act with confidence.

⑤ Positive Power Tarot

Despite our best intentions, not every day is going to go according to plan. Some days are tough "life lesson" days filled with challenging episodes. On these days, it's important to remember that the only constant in life is change. Nothing remains the same. Hard times don't last forever. New opportunities arise every minute of every day, sometimes in strange and unexpected guises, so pay attention! You can change your trajectory by seizing these moments. You can do it consciously, deliberately, and on the spot.

Don't feel like you have the power to change your day or your mood? You do! Your tarot deck can be an ally and guide when it comes to bringing uplifting, inspiring, and positive energy back into a day that's gone off track.

Before you begin, take a minute to release some of the stress and tension you're holding. Settle yourself into the right mood to receive guidance. We're going to do this with a short breathwork practice paired with a mood-lifting meditation.

We are powered by breath. We breathe in and out about 22,000 times a day. Our bodies are designed to release 70 percent of toxins through breathing. Breathing is a cleansing, renewing action available to us twenty-four hours a day. Each breath presents another opportunity to start anew, bring fresh energy in, and send old energy out. Fourfold breathing is a popular method of super-cleansing our bodies and bringing our focus back to a neutral place.

Fourfold breathing recognizes there are four phases to our breath and makes us aware of them. The four phases are:

inhaling,
lungs full,
exhaling, and
lungs empty

Aim to make these four phases of equal duration (try four seconds). When you try this, do it for at least four cycles. You will feel your body fall into alignment, feel relaxed, and feel alert. Once you've completed your four cycles, return your breath to normal and do this mood-changing meditation before drawing your card.

Mood-Lifting Meditation

Close your eyes and picture a comfortable little room inside your head. This is your private study, apothecary, temple, or sacred space, and it is filled with fascinating items. Your eyes are on a window in a distant wall of that room, a window to the world.

It is quiet and still in here. Any distracting noises or thoughts are like birds flying past that distant window. Release them without care.

There is a skylight above you, and a soft beam of white light shines down on your head. It holds you gently in its beam. Light flows in through your breath, moves through your nose, and makes its way down your body.

Allow that energy to flow where it's needed. Just breathe deeply.

On each exhale, gently release all that does not serve your highest good. Blow it away.

Inhale the light and let it cleanse your entire body, mind, spirit, and aura until you are softly glowing with that healing, soothing light yourself.

When you feel relaxed and at peace, wiggle your fingers and toes, clench and unclench your fists, and open your eyes.

Pull Your Card

Now, ask for guidance. Ask for a message that you can focus on right now, in this moment.

Pull your card and read its interpretation. Focus on the things that resonate, inspire, or touch a nerve. This guidebook includes a reassurance, an affirmation, and suggested actions for every tarot card in the deck. Zoom in on the one that feels the most relevant or inspiring for this moment. See the card you pulled as a coach, telling you how it's going and what to do in order to optimize your mood and emotional state for the rest of the day.

6 Tarot Wind Down

Your evening wind down is an important part of your day, a ritualistic time for reflection and for processing the day's events. Bathing is not only probably the easiest form of self-care, but, when regularly incorporated into your evening routine, it can provide a practical means of setting aside time to recover from and reflect on your day. In this evening bathing ritual, you will be using your tarot cards as a focus for meditation or contemplation so you can process the day's events and prepare your body and mind for a healing sleep.

In ancient Greece, people built sleep temples (called *Asclepieia*, after the Greek god of medicine) where visitors bathed in warm water, in darkness, as a means of entering a trance state, helping them to relax, heal, and overcome all manner of ailments. Think of your evening bath as a visit to your own healing sleep temple. Water is soothing and shape-shifting. It massages your muscles, stimulating circulation, bringing healing nutrients to the tissues, and helping to remove lactic acid and other waste products.

Aromatherapy can be a nice companion to this experience. Blend your own essential oils to create a scent elixir that makes your bath feel extra soothing. Lavender, marjoram, ylang-ylang, lemon, Roman chamomile, frankincense, neroli, and rose are all noted for their relaxation properties. Prepare your elixir ahead of time so it is ready to go when you're ready to step into the tub.

Adjust the light in the bathroom so that it's dark or dimly lit, ideally by candles. Place purifying, transmuting, or healing crystals (e.g., selenite, clear quartz, opal, black obsidian, onyx, jet) around the edge of your bathtub to help harmonize the vibrations in the room and bring you in line with their energy. If you don't have a bathtub, you can replicate this ritual with a foot bath.

Fill the tub with warm water and add any oils, salts, or herbs you like. When the bath is ready, strip off your clothes and submerge yourself in the water. As you settle in, notice your physical body starting to unwind and unfold in the heat and the scent of the lapping waters. Work your attention around your body, clenching and unclenching each part, releasing any tension, and noticing if there is any lingering strain or stiffness. When you find such a spot, breathe into it, massage it, and focus on letting it sag, feel heavy, and relax.

When you feel you are physically relaxed, turn your attention to your tarot cards. (It helps to have a bath tray you can keep them on, along with a little towel so you don't get them wet!)

Consider your current inner landscape—what's here this evening? What might you wish to mentally or emotionally relax, release, or heal during this bath? Possible questions to ask your deck during this ritual include the following:

What should I be grateful for as today draws to a close?
What about myself should I show love and appreciation for today?
Where in my psyche do I need to receive healing energy after today?
What do I need to release and let go of during this time out?
What wishes can I start to make for tomorrow?

Shuffle your cards as you think about your question and then pull your card. Place it on your tray or at the side of your bath—somewhere you can comfortably keep it in clear view. Let your gaze go soft, take a deep breath, and close your eyes with the card's image held in your mind's eye. Imagine that you are inside the card looking around the scene depicted on it, sitting quietly in the tableau. Ask your subconscious to receive the wisdom of this card and apply it to your question. Ask for a message. Be open to whatever images, symbols, words, ideas, or emotions flit across your mind's eye or enter your head during this quiet reflection.

Let this daydreaming continue for as long as you're happy to relax in the water. When you feel you have an answer or an idea to take with you into the next part of your evening, open your eyes and finish bathing. You can even keep your card tucked onto your bathroom mirror to remind you of its message in the morning.

⑦ Dreams of Tarot

From ancient Eastern cultures to contemporary Western science, dream analysis and interpretation has always preoccupied human attention. Yet the exact nature of dreams and the reason for our dreaming defy explanation, even now. One common view is that dreaming functions as a process of emotional and psychological healing. Our subconscious picks up elements from our day—our memories, our triggers—and presents them to us as stories that carry messages about which aspect of our lives require greater attention during our waking hours. In dreams, symbols, people, actions, scenery, moods, and conversations can all represent something else. Everything is worthy of consideration. Your subconscious is trying to talk to you.

Your tarot cards can be an ally and a tool for analysis when it comes to your dreams. With this one-card ritual, you can use them to help unlock the secrets of your subconscious.

Prepare for Sleep

This tarot reading begins before you go to sleep. Place a notepad and pen at your bedside when you get into bed so you can record your dreams when you wake up. As you settle down for the night, consider anything that happened during the day that you'd like your subconscious to work on, find answers to, provide a solution for, or process and heal. This will form the basis of your question for this reading. Once you have your question, idea, or request clearly formulated in your mind, repeat it out loud three times so that your body has consciously emitted, heard, and absorbed it. You're now ready to sleep—and dream.

You might like to take a tarot card with you on this particular journey into the dream realm—one whose energy, affirmation, or meaning resonates with what's on your mind or one that feels like a protective presence. The Empress, Queen of Cups, and The High Priestess are good cards for this. Place the card next to your bedside so that it is present if you wake up in the night. The card will watch over your dreaming self, like a guardian, and help your subconscious to respond to your needs.

Analyze Your Dreams

If you wake up and can remember a dream, grab your notepad and pen and write it all down immediately (as the brain rapidly forgets dream details). Everything is valid—scenery, storyline, characters, emotions and sensations, objects, personal associations or memories, conversations, weather, symbols, and so on. Write down whatever is clear in your mind after your dream. Most importantly, write down how you felt in your mind and body when you awoke. Our dreamt emotions often spill over to our waking self, which can be unsettling. The more you practice writing your dreams down, the more your mind will be trained to remember the details, and the better analysis you can do.

Your dream's meaning doesn't come directly from the images in the dream. Instead, you determine the meaning by analyzing how you responded to events in the dream or by considering what elements of the dream symbolically represent to you. Think of your dreaming self as an alter ego, a dream version of you. Examine what your dream self felt in response to the dream's events. Examine your dream self's response to threats, pleasure, and stimulus. Consider if anything correlates (even in an abstract way) to anything in your daily life. Zoom in on the absurd, fantastic, or abstract details and ask yourself what they represent to you. Did you behave differently in the dream than you think you would in real life? Examine the reality gaps. It might be interesting to ponder what you'd like to have changed about the dream if you could and if this desire correlates to your real life too.

You are trying to reach a conclusion—even if it feels abstract, whimsical, out-of-nowhere, or forced—about what this dream is trying to get you to address in your real life. Create a hypothesis. Write it down alongside your dream recollection.

With this initial assessment complete, turn to your tarot cards. Shuffle the cards with your hypothesis in mind. Ask for guidance. Ask how you can implant change into the day ahead, how you can make the first step, and how you can take positive action right here and now to answer your dream's (and therefore subconscious's) needs.

Draw your card. Write down its challenge and the things it suggests you do today. Simply, this is what you need to do to answer your subconscious's requests, needs, and demands.

You now possess knowledge of the action you're going to take today as a result of your dream. You are a dream analyst!

8 Tarot for Deep Reflection

Wisdom begins at the end. It's in hindsight that we glean the lessons of our experiences and form a narrative that makes sense and smooths out the ups and downs of our life path. Life is lived forward, but understanding comes by looking backward, reviewing what has happened, and seeing patterns, narratives, themes, learnings, and insights. Tarot can be a fantastic ally in this process. It can help accelerate you toward wisdom and away from pain, suffering, or confusion.

The following meditation and card draw should be conducted during times when you feel a pull toward reflection—such as when you have been through a tumultuous or transformative phase and want to understand more about its impact on your life and the new position you're in. Maybe in the past you experienced something traumatic or life-changing that was simply too raw for you to examine at the time, but now enough time has passed that you're ready to look again and find a different perspective.

Think about the situation you're reflecting on. It might help to jot down your memories of it, to clarify questions that still feel unanswered, and to notice the emotions that trouble you when you think about it. Before you begin the meditation, spread your tarot cards out in a fan in front of you so they're ready and waiting for you.

Now, prepare to relax. Find a comfortable position. Take long, slow breaths, and release all tension. You can help this along by clenching sections of your body (i.e., neck and shoulders, arms and hands, legs and feet, chest and stomach) as tightly as you can and then releasing them.

When you've come to a place of stillness, imagine, in your mind's eye, a blissful forest wilderness decked out in a glorious display of new growth. Imagine the leafy green canopy of trees, the musky scents of forest wildlife, and the chirruping of fluttering birds. Open your heart to becoming a part of this life-affirming natural world.

You find yourself in the middle of the forest and you notice there is a winding path stretching out in front of and behind you. This path represents the storyline of your life. The way forward is shrouded in mist and blocked by brambles and thickets. However, you can stroll backward—back to previous eras, chapters, and phases you've already walked through and moved on from.

As you turn back to your past and walk along the path, you glance into the dense forest on either side of you, observing shadowy images and scenes playing out in the mist and dappled light between the trees. These are episodes from your own life, safely replaying themselves from a distance so you can't interrupt or be bothered by them in the present. You can simply observe and engage, from a comfortable emotional distance, to glean a new lesson or perspective on what happened.

Walk along your path until you reach the chapter you wish to examine. Stay on the path, but turn and face the trees and watch the scenes unfold. As you do, the forest seems to stir to life around you. Everything is louder, brighter, more fragrant, warmer, and shimmering with latent power and energy. You inhale this life force deeply, and it nourishes your mind, body, and soul. With each inhale you sink deeper into the memory and your mind travels further into your subconscious to draw forth the message you need to hear about this memory now.

When you feel full of the forest's life force, take a final deep, slow breath and open your eyes.

Immediately pick up a tarot card from the fanned pile in front of you. Read it fully but pay close attention to the Reassurance and Life Lesson sections of the card's description. This is the message you're meant to receive. You may wish to reflect, sleep on, or journal about how this message could link to your memory. Consider the Do This section of the card's descriptions because it may contain advice about what you can physically do now to close this chapter completely and with peace of mind.

9 One-Card Tarot for Love

There's no doubt that, when it comes to tarot reading, love and relationships of all shapes, sizes, and stages are the most common questions and concerns for most clients. Affairs of the heart are irrational, emotional, and full of angst and heightened sensitivity. This makes it hard to see things clearly and to fully understand our own actions, needs, and rules. We can make excuses, feel clouded by lust or passion, and lose track of what's right or healthy for ourselves. Tarot can provide a calming, soothing balm to the fraught emotions in play and help guide a questioner through the storm. Tarot is the perfect ally for someone with love life turmoil, as the cards can reveal objective truth and provide hope for the future. Both are necessary when facing the realities of relationship ups and downs.

Friday is a great day to get down to love questions because it is named for the planet Venus, ruler over romance, affairs of the heart, and pleasure. You want Venus on your side when you're tackling questions about your love life. You may also want to make your space look romantic and pretty when you're doing a love reading. Pink or red crystals (carnelian, rose quartz, ruby, garnet, and blood-stone) will bring passion and ardor to your cards; place a red crystal on top of or multiple red crystals around your deck. Red or pink candles cast a rosy glow, and you could even pop a photo of the object of your affection next to your deck (to double down on them getting the hint!). These are not essential but can help amplify the right mood for asking a daring question.

Here is a list of possible one-card questions you could ask your tarot cards. Pick whichever resonate with you and align with your situation (probably no more than three). Simply jot them down. Shuffle your cards and draw a card for each question.

How can I attract my ideal partner?
What type of traits should I avoid when looking for a partner?
Where am I most likely to find the love of my life?
Is my crush drawn to me?
What steps do I need to take to attract true love?
How can I be more confident when looking for love?
When will I find my true love?
How can I get over this breakup?

Why can't I let go of this ex?
What life lesson could I learn from this recent breakup?
How can I strengthen my relationship with my partner?
What past issues are affecting my current relationship?
How can I be a better partner?
Why is my marriage struggling?
What are the threats to my relationship?
What can I do to save my relationship?
What's something I do not see in my current relationship?
How can I bring happiness back into my relationship?
In what areas does my partner need more of my support?
How can I be more in tune with my partner's feelings?
What habits need to change within this relationship?
How have I been sabotaging my relationship?
What should I know about my relationship?
What is my path to a happy and successful relationship?
How do I know if my current partner is marriage material?
How can I stop falling prey to negative patterns in my relationship?
Where is my relationship headed?
What does my love life have in store this month/year?
How have my previous relationships made me a stronger and better partner?
What's holding me back from committing?
What will happen if I get back together with my ex?
Is my current partner the right one?
Would my crush be a good potential match with me?
Will I get over my fear of love?
Is there any chance that my ex and I will ever get back together?

⑩ One-Card Tarot for Career

After love and relationships, career is probably the area that inspires the most questions during tarot readings. Some people are lucky enough to have a calling, to feel compelled toward one area of expertise, and devote their lives to it wholeheartedly, finding success and rewards across the decades. But these folks are rare; most of us take a more meandering path through our career. We drift, find our way on the job, change course, reinvent ourselves, suffer enormous doubt, find some success, experience some failure, and so on. Most people are constantly asking themselves, "Am I on the right path?" Even when the going is good, career management and planning are tricky. Our levels of confidence, creativity, health, and circumstance can all impact our hopes (and fears) for our work life and financial security.

Saturday is a great day to consider matters of career because it is named for the planet Saturn, ruler over duty, responsibility, material wealth, security, and hard work. You want Saturn on your side when tackling career issues. Additionally, you may wish to keep a career-enhancing crystal in your hand as you clarify your question and pull a card. Blue lapis lazuli and turquoise are both inspiring, motivating stones that can help you aim high and have confidence in your ability. Green chrysoprase is useful when you're seeking a new role or changing career direction. It helps to make finding work easier. A clear crystal, such as quartz, can help clear stagnant energies and attract fresh opportunities. You might consider keeping your crystal with you after the reading, especially when you're putting the tarot's advice into action, as a talisman of your good intentions and hopes.

It's good practice to ask questions about your career regularly, maybe every New Moon (a great time of the month for activation and initiation). So often, we just carry on until something unpleasant or bad happens at work and we want a change. At that point, our confidence and creativity are not great, and it's (ironically) not the best time to ideate, apply, change course, or reinvent. Do it when you're on a roll, on a high, winning. Success attracts success.

Here is a list of possible one-card career-oriented questions you could ask your tarot cards. Pick whichever resonate with you and align with your situation (I recommend no more than three at a time). Simply jot them down. Shuffle

your cards and draw a card for each. Here are some possible questions you might ask:

What kind of career area will be most fulfilling for me?
When should I change jobs?
When should I start retraining?
When should I seek promotion?
What can I do right now to help further my career?
How can I improve at my job?
How can I better communicate with my boss or employer?
What parts of my work do I love?
What kind of workplace leader could I become?
How can I balance my career with my personal life?
What could I change to enjoy my job more?
What am I not seeing about my career choices right now?
Will I succeed with this career ambition?
What are my weaknesses in my career?
What are my key strengths?
What obstacle or issue must I address?
How can I showcase and amplify my strengths at work?
What can I work on to improve my skills and capability?
What is blocking me from achieving my full potential?
How can I address the workplace problem I am facing right now?
How can I resolve conflict with my colleague?
What kind of work makes me feel useful?
What kind of work can bring me the most money?
What will happen if I stay in this role?
Who can help me in my career development right now?
What kind of mentor or coach do I need?
What should I ask for at work?

⑪ Trance Tarot

Your tarot cards can be a great partner for your meditation practice or for when it's time to turn inward and receive wisdom from your subconscious or psyche. The following meditation takes inspiration from the ancient oracle at Delphi, Pythia, the high priestess of the Temple of Apollo. Pythia shared predictions, divinations, and prophecies that she received from the god Apollo while in a trance induced by vapors that rose from a chasm in the rock beneath the temple. Pythia was among the most powerful women of the classical Greek world, and she was consulted by kings, nobles, and pilgrims. In this practice, you'll be re-creating your own oracle at home, using tarot cards and a little imagination!

Use the following meditation when you wish to receive a message, an inspiration, an intuition, or a random nudge from your psyche. Instead of relying on vapors and frenzies to stimulate insights like Pythia did, turn your focus inward and place your awareness on the inner pulsations that are visible behind your closed eyes. They will serve as your anchor as you plunge into the depths of yourself and see what lies there.

If you wish to borrow a little more inspiration from Pythia, hold or sit near psychic-enhancing crystals and rocks such as labradorite, amethyst, lapis lazuli, serpentine, clear quartz, or black obsidian. You can also light some fragrant incense or use a diffuser to create vapor. The following fragrances are associated with igniting or amplifying psychic ability: frankincense, honeysuckle, jasmine, lotus, peppermint, rose, sage, sandalwood, and vanilla.

Trance Meditation

To begin, choose a card from your deck. This card will be the anchor for your trance, vision, and message. Read the interpretation carefully and zoom in on what resonates with you the most, what seems to be speaking to you about your life right now, what provokes an emotion, or what prompts a further question. Hold on to this reaction and close your eyes.

Get comfortable in a seated position with your back straight. Focus on aligning your body: Level your pelvis, lift your chest, roll your shoulders down, and lift your head up. Place your hands on your lap.

Say to yourself, softly, "I am turning inward to explore my consciousness and receive a message."

Follow your breathing for a few minutes, inhaling and exhaling with slow, steady breaths.

Close your eyes and become aware of your inner eyes by focusing on whatever you see on your closed eyelids. You can stimulate visions by squinting and squeezing your eyes a few times and moving your eyeballs around. You are now observing your own inner world.

Your inner world might appear as a spectrum of color, a shifting plane of shadows, a night sky, a pulsating field, or something else. What you see doesn't matter as much as your desire to read symbols, shapes, forms, and messages in it. You are looking at your inner consciousness—the source of sensations, perceptions, emotions, and ideas.

Let your mind play over your response to the tarot card you pulled and notice the dynamic of your vision changing or shifting. What vibrations, expansions, blurring, new colors, shapes, silhouettes, or images appear? What do they make you feel or sense or think?

Take as much time as you need to follow the patterns of the designs that are a part of your inner world awareness. When you notice you are following an irrelevant train of thought, simply bring your awareness back to looking behind your eyelids.

Maybe you can see an even deeper, denser inner spot of awareness in the mosaic. Focus there, letting it beckon you ever deeper into your subconscious and your mind's workings. Be still. Observe.

When you feel you've received the message, image, emotion, or understanding you were looking for, bring your focus back to your breath and follow the inhalation and exhalation with your mind. Wiggle your fingers and toes, prepare to return to the waking world, shift your weight, and open your eyes.

It's a good idea to write everything down right away. Don't worry if some of it does not make sense or seem coherent; write it down anyway. Return to these notes later or the following day. Let your subconscious continue to ruminate on what you received. Keep the card you drew close by to you. An inspiration will emerge!

⑫ Other Side Tarot

An inescapable hard truth is that the longer we live, the more people we lose along the way. The late Queen Elizabeth II once wisely observed that "grief is the price we pay for love." Everyone deals with death and grief individually, and different cultures have their own guiding beliefs and rituals. Nevertheless, I think everyone feels a universal need to stay close to their loved ones on the "other side" and to remember, reflect on, and even converse with them.

Tarot can provide a conduit for receiving messages from your loved ones who've passed on. It can be as simple as thinking about your loved one, asking for a message from them, and then pulling a card.

If you're seeking a deeper experience or if you struggle to feel a connection, the following meditation can help you travel inward to a more liminal, dream-like space where it is easier to connect with those from the other side.

Connecting with the Other Side Meditation

If you have a photo of, memento from, or possession that belonged to your loved one, keep it near you for this meditation. Before you begin, fan the tarot cards in front of you.

Close your eyes and breathe deeply and evenly. Focus on relaxing every part of your body, from your head, jaw, neck, and shoulders down through your torso and arms and into your legs and feet.

Put one or both of your hands on your heart and imagine a glowing, gold beam of light connecting you to your loved one in spirit. This tie is unbreakable, eternal, and always present, even when you're not thinking of your loved one. From this tie, their love continues to flow into and all around you. Pause and think about this everlasting bond. If it makes you feel tearful, then let those tears flow. Tears can help you to heal. They release emotions that feel heavy.

Now imagine that you are in a dark room and all you can see is the glowing ribbon of your connection flowing from your heart and leading you into the darkness ahead. You follow the ribbon and, with each step, you feel the love inside you welling up bigger and stronger.

The pathway ahead gets lighter, and you can see shadows and forms on the walls around you. You keep walking and following the glowing golden thread.

Suddenly your vision clears, the space lightens, and there ahead of you, with their back to you, is your loved one. They are waiting for you. As you call their name, they turn and open their arms to you. You embrace, and the surge of love and joy you feel at being able to touch, hold, see, smell, and speak to them again is overwhelming.

During your embrace, they whisper something in your ear. It's something they want you to know about your life right now. This is a piece of wisdom or advice that they have crossed through the veil to impart. It is precious and useful, and it is going to help you.

Stay as long as you wish with your loved one. Say whatever you need to say. When you feel their strength is ebbing, step away, bid them farewell for now, and open your eyes. Pick a card from the fan spread in front of you.

This card, along with what you discussed in your vision, is your personal message from your departed loved one. Savor it, and keep it out for the day. If you're struggling to make a connection with it, think about your person's life and whether the situation/energy of that card is something they may have faced. They could be trying to draw your attention to a life lesson they have already learned and can impart. Let their life story teach you.

Card Interpretations for ONE-CARD DRAWS

———— ✕ ————

0 The Fool

Advice for Right Now/Today Be positive, proactive, optimistic, and enthusiastic. Activate a major new beginning in your life. Turn the page. Write a new story. Clean slate. Fresh start. You may not feel ready (no one ever does), but don't let that stop you. Others may disapprove or disagree with your idea or plan—ignore them! It's time to make a bold leap. Do it today!

Affirmation I am embracing a fresh start.

A Reassurance No pressure. Nothing has to be right first time; this is all a learning curve. And, if something goes awry, well then it becomes wisdom and life experience. Set off and learn a new pathway without overthinking it or worrying about the outcome right now.

Life Lesson Life is full of new beginnings. Some are done to us; some are of our own doing. This beginning can be of your own doing—make that so. Be the doer instead of the done-to.

A Challenge Think about the new beginning you most yearn to activate, the one you daydream about, and make an overt move in its direction today. Or actually make the leap altogether!

Do This Begin afresh. Take the uncharted path. Be different.

Don't Do This Cling to the past. Stick with the same old same old. Refuse to embark on something new for fear of reprisals or failure.

Who? Aquarians. People who are inspiring and enthusiastic. People who urge or trigger you to make a fresh start or activate something new.

When? Spring. Late January or February.

Is This a Yes or a No? A major yes. Go for it and enjoy the ride. Set off no matter what and do this for you, no matter what others say.

1 The Magician

Advice for Right Now/Today Exercise your will and act. Create. Make a cunning plan and execute it, using your own wiliness and smart thinking. Make something new, invent something, or bring something new into the world. Use and refine your talents. Consciously use your strengths to manifest a new reality. You have power. Use it today.

Affirmation I am harnessing the wild magic within me for my own ends.

A Reassurance You have everything you need. You are ready to create, innovate, manifest, and bring forth what you've got into the world. It's time.

Life Lesson Never compare yourself to others. You are unique and incomparable. You need to discover, reveal, amplify, and rely on your own inner, wild magic and creativity. It's all there.

A Challenge What talent did you enjoy or feel at home with during your child-hood? Go back to look at what you used to do well, easily and naturally—what you were complimented on and what brought joy. It's all still there and can be reinvented in your adult realm.

Do This Create. Write. Draw. Design. Make. Grow. Invent. Learn. Manifest.

Don't Do This Use your skills for shady ends! Be a bringer of shadow, not light, to the world. Move forward with motives and intentions that are not clear and transparent.

Who? Geminis and Virgos. People who are smart, shrewd, worldly, communicative, and interested in everything. Often people who are well-traveled and cultured.

When? June and September. Wednesdays.

Is This a Yes or a No? A major yes. Make your own destiny, take charge, and create a new storyline.

II The High Priestess

Advice for Right Now/Today Tune in to your spide-y senses, your psychic twinkle, and your gut instinct, and notice what they are telling you. Don't ignore those feelings. Make sure you have space today to meditate, ruminate, think, day-dream, and ideally journal what you experience. Try to connect the dots and find a message. Pay close attention to déjà vu, coincidences, dreams, and serendipity. The Universe is presenting you with information in a secretive, subconscious way today.

Affirmation I am listening to and trusting my subconscious.

A Reassurance Deep down, you have the answers and you know the truth. Deep down, you understand it all. It's just a matter of being quiet and still enough for this information to emerge as knowledge and solid ideas.

Life Lesson We are all gifted with an inner sat nav—that is, our intuition. It tells us the truth about situations, people, opportunities, and places. Learn to recognize your own intuitive voice and how it talks to you, and trust it more often. You know, deep down, much more than your chatterbox brain likes to imagine.

A Challenge Take twenty minutes out of today's schedule to meditate. Ask your-self, "What does my subconscious want me to know today?" Lie down, close your eyes, breathe deeply and evenly, and let your imagination wander. Let thoughts come and go, and let images, ideas, memories, and questions pass by on the big screen of your mind's eye.

Do This Pause to think, look inward, trust your intuition, and pay attention to signs, omens, and coincidences.

Don't Do This Rush or push ahead with something you know there's a red flag waving over or something that your gut doesn't feel settled about. Don't push down uncomfortable feelings, but process, question, and release them.

Who? Cancerians. People who are extremely spiritual, knowing, intuitive, or even psychic. Mentors, gurus, creatives, and teachers.

When? Any significant moon phases (Full, New, eclipse). Late June and July. Mondays.

Is This a Yes or a No? It's a pause button. Take a moment to truly connect with your gut instinct, intuition, and hunches. Trust them. Go with their response.

III The Empress

Advice for Right Now/Today This card represents fertility, mothering, passion, family, life force, and nature. Take it back to basics or the fundamentals—the things that matter most to making you feel loved, taken care of, and part of something in this world. Respect life. Be good to yourself and others. Practice self-care. Show love. Receive love.

Affirmation I am surrounded by unconditional love and natural beauty.

A Reassurance You are loved, needed, respected, and valued. You make a difference. Others want your company, time, and attention, and you can offer these things anytime, any day, for free without negatively impacting yourself.

Life Lesson The best things in life are free. At the end, in the end, we revel and dwell on the happy memories we've made with others (not work, or money, or possessions). Every day presents a new opportunity to make more magical, loving memories with others.

A Challenge Consider how good you are to your family, loved ones, friends, colleagues, neighbors, and community. Is there someone you could make a positive difference to today?

Do This Call up family, do someone a favor, go for a walk someplace beautiful, show love and care for others, reflect on the simple pleasures in your life, or consider if it's the right time to grow your family or get a pet.

Don't Do This Harbor anger, resentment, regret, or bitterness. These emotions only eat you up inside. Practice self-love and self-care, and start by releasing negative feelings. Start today kind.

Who? Taureans and Librans. Family, especially mothers or nurturing figures. People with whom you feel sexual passion or chemistry.

When? Fridays. Late April through May and late September through October.

Is This a Yes or a No? A yes. Follow your heart, follow your passion, and do what feels right to you.

IV The Emperor

Advice for Right Now/Today Take charge, take control, and take ownership of your goals and agenda. Make a plan and execute it single-mindedly, even ruthlessly. No one is going to enact your will for you; it has to come from you and you alone. Shake off any unhealthy power dynamics in the relationships in your life. Stand tall and independent and resolute.

Affirmation I am taking control of my own destiny today.

A Reassurance You are the designer, the creator, and the executor of your destiny. Even feeling passive or unwilling to make a decision is still an action. Seek to be self-serving, positive, and proactive. Be the doer, not the done-to.

Life Lesson If you don't consciously create, write, direct, and play the leading role in the story of your own life, then you will get sucked into someone else's drama.

A Challenge Are you putting off, delaying, projecting, excusing, or waiting for someone else to take charge, make it happen, or do it for you? Are you hoping external events will solve your problems? Stop. Take charge and responsibility yourself. Today!

Do This Feel your own power. Make your own plan. Act it out with confidence and courage. Reward yourself afterward. Go again!

Don't Do This Hope for others to rescue or save you. Wait and see. Hold back and let someone else take over or make the big decisions.

Who? Aries. Father figures. Bosses. People who are overbearing, authoritative, a little joyless, pedantic, and obsessed with rules.

When? Tuesdays. Late March through April.

Is This a Yes or a No? A yes if it's what *you* want. The only question here is whether you truly, authentically, deep down want this yourself. If there is any outside pressure or expectation, then examine it more closely.

V The Hierophant

Advice for Right Now/Today Trust in your own power, draw it forth, and manifest. And if you can't, find help to support you in making that happen. Move beyond technique to actual practice. Step to the next level of your chosen game. The Hierophant is a spiritual guru, a mentor, a teacher, and a master. Consider how you relate to that role: Is this you, as you are now? Are you seeking this person? Or are you perhaps under the undue influence of this person?

Affirmation I am learning by challenging and practicing what I learn.

A Reassurance You never have to try and do it all alone. You can join an organization, institution, group, or forum. You can seek a mentor, coach, or teacher. And eventually you will move into that role yourself, sharing what you have learned and passing on your wisdom.

Life Lesson Eventually every apprentice overtakes their master. Understand that truth because you will likely experience it from both ends.

A Challenge Consider where you need a teacher, where you yourself can teach others, and where you might wish to resist or overturn the doctrines or teachings you grew up with.

Do This Seek a mentor or coach. Take a class. Join a spiritual group or circle. Practice something esoteric. Challenge a tradition in your realm.

Don't Do This Mindlessly carry on doing what you've been taught when you no longer think it serves you well or makes sense in your life.

Who? Taureans. Mentors, coaches, teachers, gurus, or advisors. People who are wise, spiritual, and willing to give freely. People you respect and wish to learn from.

When? Fridays. Late April through May.

Is This a Yes or a No? Yes, if this aligns with your conscience and moral compass. You might wish to meditate or pray on the matter.

VI The Lovers

Advice for Right Now/Today Align your physical body, heart, and mind to prioritize what (or who) your true passion is right now, because you might be feeling confused. We are fickle creatures, we can be drawn to more than one thing at any one time, and we fall prey to temptations. Tune in to your physical attraction, your heart's feelings of love, and your thoughts. Line them up, know your priorities, and act accordingly.

Affirmation I am working out what and whom I love.

A Reassurance It's normal to feel drawn to someone new, even if you're in love with someone else. Temptation is a part of life. Your job is to work out what to do about it, how to act, and what's important. It's okay to end an old relationship and start a new one. It's okay to feel tempted but resist and refocus on what you have. Make up your mind.

Life Lesson In love, play the long game and keep Lady Karma off your case by treating others as you'd like to be treated yourself.

A Challenge If you feel attraction to someone or something else other than your chosen one (it could be a friend, role, or project, too, not necessarily a romantic interest), question what this new attraction represents, why it tempts you, and what it promises. Deconstruct the feeling.

Do This Consider consequences and act consciously. Be fair. Know what you want most.

Don't Do This Hedge your bets, play both sides, lie, cheat, or activate a double existence that will eventually overwhelm and possibly destroy you.

Who? Geminis. People you are irresistibly attracted to (even if you feel you shouldn't be). People who blow hot and cold, mess around with you, or are unclear about their intentions.

When? Wednesdays. Late May through June.

Is This a Yes or a No? Unclear. This card is very ambiguous and full of conflict. Pause until you experience genuine clarity here.

VII The Chariot

Advice for Right Now/Today Action with intent. Momentum. Focused tactics executed and driven by a robust vision and strategy. Today is all about purposeful and direct movement in the direction of a chosen goal. Travel may also be very relevant, whether it's your method of transport, new journeys, an inspiring outing, a holiday, a move of home, or even a location change. You are on the move.

Affirmation I have the plan, the willpower, and the determination to succeed.

A Reassurance Today is a day when you will just know what you want to do, why, and how. The stars will align. Use this purposeful energy to make progress, take strides, and change your position. Move closer to your goals; the Universe is backing you.

Life Lesson Without a purpose or destination, our efforts and movements can lead to very little, a spiral or circling of the same space and territory over and over. Set goals. Align your actions to your goals and get ahead.

A Challenge Think about your place in this world (from your physical home or location to your status or role in the pecking order to your travel goals). Are you where you want to be? If not, what can you do about it right now? You have control over where you're at and where you're heading, so exercise this power deliberately.

Do This Execute a plan. Set a goal. Book a trip or holiday. Consider moving (in order to achieve a bigger goal).

Don't Do This Fall into the schemes and plotlines of another's life story. Stay in the same place or position for the sake of it or for no positive reason.

Who? Cancerians. People who are travelers, in transit, or new to your realm. People who are connected to transport, live overseas, or are on some kind of journey or outing. People with purpose.

When? Mondays. New or Full Moons. Late June through July.

Is This a Yes or a No? Yes. Forge ahead with purpose and intent. Be bold.

VIII Strength

Advice for Right Now/Today Use the subtler shades of your strength when approaching today's to-do list. Don't be the roaring lion (unless it really calls for it; you do have this baser and more fundamental aggressor within you, if needed). Consider wisdom, courage, confidence, persuasion, compassion, patience, resilience, influence, and stoicism. Soft often overcomes hard (think of water and its relentless, smooth, wearing force).

Affirmation I am persuasive, influential, and resolute.

A Reassurance You have everything you need today. You have a broader range of soft skills than you realize. You have an assertive voice; use it today and see how much you can achieve without resorting to force or fight.

Life Lesson It is through facing, overcoming, and understanding our challenges that we grow the most and the fastest. Welcome the daily challenges of life. See them as a task master or teacher. Learn the lessons.

A Challenge Practice your assertive (instead of your passive or aggressive) voice today. Look for opportunities to speak up and out, with clarity but also understanding. Allow room for dissent or challenge. Listen well. Absorb new ideas. Reach a mutual place of understanding. Use every conversation as a practice zone.

Do This Stick up for yourself. Tackle a long-standing challenge. Be assertive. Use your softer skills to persuade or influence someone or something.

Don't Do This Unleash your teeth and claws at the first provocation or because you feel scared. You must overcome your fear, be calm, and be led by your strongest self.

Who? Leos. People who enter your life to impart some kind of personal growth, lesson, or development (from a positive or negative place). People who are here to support you through hardship.

When? Sundays. Late July through August.

Is This a Yes or a No? Yes. This path will bring some hardship and need for personal growth, but you can handle it.

IX The Hermit

Advice for Right Now/Today It's important to seek solitude today and to be alone with yourself and your thoughts. It's a good day to wrestle with a task or issue that requires concentration and focus. You have the right energy to do that today, and you will make important progress. Sometimes we have to travel within to find answers. Sometimes we have to rely on me, myself, and I.

Affirmation I am seeking enlightenment and knowledge.

A Reassurance You don't need to have all the answers right now—just, perhaps, the right questions. It takes time and energy to work out the answers, which is okay because you have both. You don't need help. You just need to trust yourself.

Life Lesson Life is primarily a solo journey, even though we encounter and travel with others along the way. We all have to learn to be by ourselves, rely on ourselves, and answer our own unanswered questions. That is the path of maturing and becoming a master of your own destiny, a leader instead of someone who is led.

A Challenge Focus on the challenge, problem, or task that requires your attention. Clear some space and time to get your head into it and tackle the outstanding questions or issues.

Do This Seek solitude. Think. Research. Probe. Ask for enlightenment and meditate. Feed your subconscious with a new stimulus and then let it reveal the answers.

Don't Do This Distract yourself with company, socializing, or frivolous details or projects.

Who? Virgos. Students, academics, teachers, philosophers, learned colleagues, or those who seek solitude with which to pursue their education and enlightenment.

When? Wednesdays. Late August through September.

Is This a Yes or a No? Yes, if it is an informed decision based on the best of what you know right now. If there are unanswered questions you can answer, then figure them out first.

X The Wheel Of Fortune

Advice for Right Now/Today Change is the only constant in life. That wheel of fortune never stops spinning; our fortunes are always changing. Recognize this today and enjoy the ride, whether you're heading up or down. Don't let success go to your head, and don't let failure go to your heart. Better still, activate one major change in your direct circle of influence today. Something significant.

Affirmation I choose to change my life one step at a time, and today I make that step.

A Reassurance Everything is going to be alright in the end, so when things don't feel right, it just means it's not the end yet. Keep going.

Life Lesson We all fear change. We all gravitate to the familiar. But we must all learn to accept, then embrace, and then proactively seek change, growth, and progress. Being comfortable with and positive about change makes life so much easier.

A Challenge If you are facing a crossroads anywhere in your life, take the untraveled path today. Opt for change. If not, why have you reached this crossroads at all?

Do This Make a bold leap. Take a risk. Do the unexpected thing. Take the new option. Activate a transformation.

Don't Do This Stick to the tried and tested same old same old for the sake of it. Be frightened of something, someplace, or someone new. Suppress or avoid new opportunities.

Who? Sagittarians and Pisceans. People who provoke change or transformation in your realm. People who stimulate and inspire or even trigger you.

When? Thursdays. Late November through December and late February through March.

Is This a Yes or a No? Yes . . . but then expect the unexpected. Change will trigger yet more change.

XI Justice

Advice for Right Now/Today Be super sensitive to matters relating to the concept of justice today, be they literal manifestations such as legal situations, contracts, or administrative negotiations or more abstract notions such as how you are treating someone else or how they are treating you. Always act like Lady Karma is watching (she is) and do what you think a higher self would advise. Stay on the straight and narrow, and be a force for good today.

Affirmation I am a force for truth, justice, and positivity in my corner of Earth today.

A Reassurance Everything tends to shake out the right way in the end. Lady Karma has a long memory and, even if events don't conspire to reward or punish the players, the conscience has a way of pricking us. Be good. Be fair. Be just.

Life Lesson Everyone does what they do because they think it's right. Most people believe they're doing the right thing. The trouble is, we all have moral blind spots and weigh the odds much more heavily in our own favor. Be mindful of your blind spots. Be honest about your intentions.

A Challenge Look at a situation you think is unfair (to you or to someone else) and think about it from the perspective of the person or institution inflicting the unfairness. What do you see? What might their blind spot be? If you want to persuade them, you need to understand their position and speak to their priorities and values.

Do This Be truthful. Be fair. Be supportive. Be analytical. Look at your own actions and intentions with brutal honesty. Forgive others.

Don't Do This Take the shortcut or path of least resistance when you know, deep down, that it hurts someone else or causes negativity.

Who? Librans. People associated with justice, institutions, education, or truth in your realm. People who are involved in a legal, contractual, or ethical situation with you.

When? Fridays. Late September through October.

Is This a Yes or a No? It's a pause button. Take a moment to think about what the right thing to do here is. Follow your moral compass, even if it leads to a harder path.

XII The Hanged Man

Advice for Right Now/Today Take a leap into the darkness, turn things upside down, change your perspective, or look through a different lens. Focus on situations that make you feel like you've reached a limbo or a stagnated or frustrated state. If you keep on doing the same old things, you'll keep on getting the same old results. Time for a radical shift in your attitude and approach. Time to sacrifice something, someone, or your own self.

Affirmation I am seeing my realm with new eyes, and I am open to new ideas.

A Reassurance You have reached this impasse for a good reason. You are being guided toward a new, more fulfilling, more rewarding way of doing things. Sure, it might smart a little to think you have been wrong in some way, but get over that; we are all wrong sometimes.

Life Lesson There's always more than one way to skin a cat. What worked for you once might not always work because circumstances, people, auras, and energies shift and change all the time. Be flexible.

A Challenge Consider what you could sacrifice today that might prove to be a catalyst for change, progress, or action. Consider making a bold leap that offers something totally different and fresh to the situation. Be different.

Do This Walk in someone else's shoes; see their point of view. Make a sacrifice. Do things differently. Seek enlightenment from opposite sources.

Don't Do This Carry on doing the same old things. Resist a new approach. Rely on tried and trusted methods.

Who? Pisceans. Somebody who represents an enigma in your realm; perhaps they are blocking you or behaving in a way you cannot understand.

When? Late February through March.

Is This a Yes or a No? It's a pause, as this card represents limbo. It's unlikely you have hit upon the right course of action just yet.

XIII Death

Advice for Right Now/Today Significant, radical, and lasting change is afoot today and heading your way. The best way to get through it and come out the other side to a place of new growth and opportunity is calm acceptance. Nothing stays still. Nothing lasts forever. Resistance is futile. Know that there's a grand plan, a purpose, and a new opportunity brewing inside every change you face. Be brave, positive, and hopeful.

Affirmation I welcome change as a positive force in my life today.

A Reassurance Nothing stands still for long, so if you don't like how things ended today then fear not, because they won't stay like that for long. And if you do like how things ended today, then savor and enjoy the moment for the same reason!

Life Lesson Everything has a dual nature. Everything has a light and dark, a positive aspect and a negative aspect. Choose to amplify the positive and mitigate the negative. When you choose to focus on the bright side (while not ignoring the tricky parts), you will feel better about everything. When you feel better, everything somehow seems easier. It's a virtuous circle.

A Challenge Notice the forces at play around you today. Lean into the influences, impacts, and shifting energies. Acknowledge them, work with them, and look for the bright side, the silver linings, and the opportunities. Better still, activate a positive change of your own and cheat the game!

Do This Make a change, accept news with good grace, look for the silver linings, make a bold leap, start a new good habit or routine, get a makeover, or look to change yourself within.

Don't Do This Cling to the old, familiar, routine, conventional way of being or doing something.

Who? Scorpios. Magnetic, charismatic, but also mysterious figures in your realm whom you admire but struggle to get close to. People who are triggering a major transformation in your life.

When? Late October through November.

Is This a Yes or a No? Yes. This card represents the death of one cycle so that a new one can arise; therefore it encourages change, movement, and action.

XIV Temperance

Advice for Right Now/Today Balance, equilibrium, harmony, and finding a grounded footing on an even keel. Find your balance today in areas of life where you have felt thrown off kilter, areas of life that have been taken to extremes, or areas where circumstances have inflicted upon you a new normal that has been difficult to get used to. The message of this card is moderation, temperance, adjustment, finding the middle path, and looking for compromise and resolution.

Affirmation I am centered, grounded, balanced, and strong.

A Reassurance You are doing great. You are going with the flow, learning from your lessons, and growing all the time. Keep going! Notice where there have been extremes or pressures around you and consciously make an adjustment for them today. Find your feet. Seek grounding. You are flexible and strong.

Life Lesson Life is like a pendulum. It swings in one direction and then the other; every action has a reaction. We spend a great deal of time learning to balance in the middle and find that stable, harmonious, strong position that enables us to withstand the continual swings. Be mindful of this process.

A Challenge Seek moderation in your life today and notice where it doesn't exist—where there's an intensity or pressure point that threatens your grounding and stability. Look to correct it, whether it's a bad habit, an unhealthy pattern, a relationship dynamic, work/life balance pressure, or an extreme expectation.

Do This Cut back on any excessive behaviors or habits. Compromise and seek resolutions. Practice grounding meditations and breathing exercises. Stand your ground. Moderate and adjust for imbalances.

Don't Do This Overdo anything! Continue with radical, unhealthy, extreme, or destabilizing attitudes, actions, or behaviors.

Who? Sagittarians. Someone who has (often quietly) impacted your life and changed how you think about things, maybe philosophically or maybe by showing you a new way.

When? Thursdays. Late November through December.

Is This a Yes or a No? Yes, if this action reflects progress, moving forward, or adapting to something new or different in your world.

XV The Devil

Advice for Right Now/Today The Devil represents our shadow side and whatever lurks there (greed, envy, shame, secret desires, narcissism, anger, etc.). It also represents the things we suppress, ignore, or deny about our own nature, often projecting them onto other poor, unfortunate souls. Today is a day to face those truths, to see and accept yourself all the way to the bottom, and to overcome or address the parts you don't like. Don't be manipulated or enslaved to your shadow side; make friends, understand, and work with it.

Affirmation I am not defined by my mistakes and wrongdoings. I choose to learn from them.

A Reassurance We all have a public face, a private one . . . and a secret one. We all harbor negative, even toxic, emotions, thoughts, and feelings. It's normal. Accept it and face it. Look into what lies beneath. Only you can understand how to overcome your own shadows.

Life Lesson Every saint has a past, and every sinner has a future. Be compassionate. Seek to understand and resolve rather than judge and scold.

A Challenge Work on your shadow side today. Do a guided meditation to meet your inner shadow/devil/demon and have a chat. Seriously! Meet them someplace neutral (mentally) and ask how they are, what they want from you, and why they feel what they feel. Illuminating insight, maybe even life-changing insight, will emerge.

Do This Be honest and transparent about how you feel. Take ownership of your actions 100 percent. Be responsible for the consequences of things you've done. Ask for forgiveness.

Don't Do This Project onto others. Deny your feelings. Lie about your sins. Carry on being enslaved by addictions or unhealthy behaviors.

Who? Capricorns. A worldly, shrewd, slightly dark and dangerous character. Someone who tempts you down a path of least resistance. Or someone who is a taskmaster in your realm, driving you to improve, do better, and live well.

When? Saturdays. Late December through January.

Is This a Yes or a No? Yes, if you accept and are prepared to own all the consequences (for yourself and others) of this choice.

XVI The Tower

Advice for Right Now/Today Get ready for a rumble, a big surprising event or revelation, or the collapse of something powerful (but fading or false) in your life. Change is afoot; new energy is flowing. Make sure you are moving in the right direction and with the flow, not against it. When all is said and done, what remains will be the firm, true foundations upon which you can redesign and rebuild your life as you want it to be. Sometimes the Universe does us a favor and ends unwanted things for us—that might happen today.

Affirmation What matters is that I can build on firm and true foundations.

A Reassurance Whatever happens today, or very soon, will be for the best. It might sting a little as it happens, but divine forces are moving around you now, conspiring to bring you events that will propel you onto the right pathway.

Life Lesson Nothing stands tall forever. The Tower will always fall. The new pushes out the old.

A Challenge Look at what you wish, privately, no longer had a hold over you or was present in your life. Are you brave enough to end this yourself or do you hope that the Universe gets involved and takes it out of your hands? You decide.

Do This Be brave. Look to the long term and act in accordance with that time-scale and your long-game ambitions and hopes. Let go of things that are false, fading, or negative. Know that everything is happening for the best. Leave things you're tired of.

Don't Do This Overreact to events. Suddenly see things that you have long despised through rose-tinted glasses just because they're in danger of disappearing.

Who? Aries and Scorpio. People who are bold, domineering, impactful, and direct. They will influence your life dramatically and significantly, for good or bad, maybe both.

When? Tuesdays. Late March through April and late October through November.

Is This a Yes or a No? No. The Tower is a warning.

XVII The Star

Advice for Right Now/Today We have always looked to the skies and heavens for hope, guidance, and inspiration, and The Star embodies that optimistic desire and wish fulfillment behavior in all of us. Basically, today is all about making a dream come true, activating a heart's desire, or stepping in the direction of something you hope and wish for. Life will bring moments of sheer joy, many times over, when you get something you truly want. Today could be that day.

Affirmation I am making my wishes come true today.

A Reassurance The Universe has got your back, believes in your goals, and is going to bring you an extra helping of good fortune and opportunity to help you along today. Put this magic to good use and prioritize working on the things that matter most.

Life Lesson The higher you aim, the better the outcome. Aim for the stars. Be led by your best hopes, not your worst fears.

A Challenge Zoom in and focus on the goal or daydream you cherish and fantasize about most often and most vividly. Take a pause to imagine what achieving this would look and feel like. Really live this fantasy. Think it, feel it, and believe it. Make a direct and bold leap in its direction today. It will pay off.

Do This Pursue a dream. Share your fantasies and ideals. Take a chance. Book that place, reserve the spot, make the offer, put in your pitch, propose to them, apply for the role, ask them out, make the deal, or share the idea.

Don't Do This Squander your time serving other people's agendas. Refuse to take a chance for fear of failure. Believe that your dreams are not worthy or valid.

Who? Aquarians. People who inspire, encourage, and enliven you, making you see the "what if's" in your world, supporting your visions and dreams, and activating a new dream to come true.

When? Late January through February.

Is This a Yes or a No? Yes. Make your proposal or action even bigger and bolder, too.

XVIII The Moon

Advice for Right Now/Today Today might feel a little strange, ethereal, or mysterious. You are in the throes of the elusive Moon, which means there are secret doorways, riddles, hidden agendas, and illusions swirling around you today. Seek truth. Ask questions. Research. Probe. Don't take things at face value today; dig a little deeper or push a little harder. Don't make any major moves or decisions until you reach truth, clarity, and a firm foundation.

Affirmation My heart only listens to the truth.

A Reassurance We have no way of knowing about or seeing into all the games, maneuvers, interactions, ploys, and schemes swirling around us, and most of it is irrelevant anyway. But every now and again, we get caught in another's web or influenced by someone else's lies or secrets. Be aware of this and know you will come through unscathed. Basically, their drama is not your issue.

Life Lesson Many things are not what they initially seem to be. Face values and first impressions are merely that—superficial and surface presentations. Always be mindful there are deeper layers and currents to every person, situation, or interaction.

A Challenge Think about something that feels a little off in your realm, a situation where you suspect there is more going on than what is being presented. Make today an opportunity to look at what lies beneath, to ask questions and find out more. Reserve judgment until you do.

Do This Research the unknown or secretive. Ask questions and probe the answers. Observe closely. Listen attentively. Consider the value and intention of actions more than words.

Don't Do This Take everything you're told at face value. Refuse to engage with your gut instincts and intuitions.

Who? Cancerians. People with secrets. Those who remain a mystery to you and whose true motivations and intentions you can't fathom . . . yet.

When? Mondays. Late June through July.

Is This a Yes or a No? No. Find out more first; answer the unanswered questions. You don't know enough just yet.

XIX The Sun

Advice for Right Now/Today Today is going to be a "best ever" kind of day. Good fortune, fresh opportunity, broadening horizons, joyful invitations, and successful ventures are all on the cards, lying in store for you. It's like entering a new life through a portal that you've been busy building. The time is right to make that bold leap and jump into your new guise, version, lifestyle, or plans. Be confident, have self-belief, and trust that this is not a flash in the pan. This is your new world, and you deserve it.

Affirmation I am successful, happy, confident, and ready.

A Reassurance Some days just shine with a warm glow in our memories, and today has that potential. Savor every moment. Make the most of every encounter and opportunity. Be positive and proactive, and you will be rewarded with more opportunity than you think is possible right now.

Life Lesson Everything in life is temporary, so when the going is good, make sure you enjoy and receive it fully.

A Challenge What is your biggest, boldest, most life-changing plan, ideal, vision, or dream? Why aren't you working on it? Make a concerted effort today to step up and make it happen. Do something proactive about it, because the Universe is backing you.

Do This Book a trip, plan a holiday, or consider a location change. Apply for a dream role. Ask out someone whom you've long admired. Tell them how you really feel. Pitch the idea.

Don't Do This Wait for validation or inspiration before making a move. Sit and pray for divine intervention.

Who? Leos. People from overseas, especially sunny and warm places. People to whom you are attracted. People who make you feel inspired and empowered when you're close to them, like they're a source of good energy and light.

When? Sundays. Late July through August.

Is This a Yes or a No? Yes. Be bold, act with confidence, and follow your heart.

XX Judgment

Advice for Right Now/Today Judgment can mean many things to different people. How does it resonate with you today? Are you fearful of being judged? Maybe keen to judge someone else? Seeking judgment yourself? It is likely that today will bring an epiphany, a piece of closure, or a new perspective on something deeply personal. Today, your own true nature is laid bare (for better or worse). Know thyself. Know thy opportunity. Celebrate being who you are, warts and all, and seek to create the niche in this world that fits you—gifts, talents, shadows, claws, and all.

Affirmation There is only one me. The only worthwhile comparison I make is my current self versus my old selves.

A Reassurance Self-awareness and knowledge can come from difficult circumstances, interactions, or behaviors. Don't shy away from being open and eager to learn when the going gets tough. This can help turn challenge into opportunity.

Life Lesson Hardship is a good teacher. We learn a lot about our nature when we are under pressure, in the wrong, or reflecting on troubles. Extract the life lesson and move along to a better version of yourself.

A Challenge Stop judging others and turn your gaze back to your own role, actions, and input in this situation. Measure your own behavior fairly and make amends if it has been lacking. Seek to learn about your nature from your behavior, and act as an impartial observer.

Do This Ask for feedback. Own who you are. Reflect on your actions. Apologize. Talk about something difficult or confusing. Read self-help or personal growth content.

Don't Do This Wallow in self-loathing or pity. Overinflate your actions. Navel gaze. Try to conform to what you think others expect, shape-shifting into a false version of yourself.

Who? Scorpios. People who have died but who meant a great deal to you, and perhaps have a message for you today. People who provoke for you an epiphany about yourself and your life.

When? Late October through November.

Is This a Yes or a No? Yes, if this aligns with your honest opinion and judgment of yourself and your situation.

XXI The World

Advice for Right Now/Today Today you will come full circle, completing a course of action that you began in innocence, gained experience from, and now get to close with a sense of renewed purity, ready to start a new journey. The World is the final card of the Major Arcana. It speaks of completion, ultimate achievement, and reaching the natural conclusion of an important cycle. It also can literally point to global travel, overseas expansion or connections, or the broadening of horizons.

Affirmation I celebrate my achievements and build on the knowledge I've earned.

A Reassurance Life never stands still. Never fear an ending or closure, because it simply sweeps away what has run its course, leaving you the space and energy to begin something new and fulfilling. This is the pattern of all life and all living things.

Life Lesson Every ending is merely the embryo of a new beginning. Life is cyclical. There is no final destination, so keep ebbing and flowing. Be hopeful.

A Challenge Consider the areas of your life (family, home, work, friends, etc.) and categorize them according to life cycle. Where are you just starting out? Where are you midway through, struggling with an obstacle? Where are you nearing a milestone, reaching a conclusion, or ready to release? When you ask yourself these questions, notice how things run in cycles. They never end; they just keep renewing and repeating. Be conscious of this.

Do This Review and reflect on something nearing completion. Celebrate success. Categorize the life cycle stages in your realm. Think about what's next and start ideating and researching. Book a trip overseas. Broaden your global horizons, contacts, and connections.

Don't Do This Cling to things that are reaching their natural conclusion. Be fearful of the future and feel as though you have no control.

Who? Capricorns. People who provoke ambition, goal-setting, and progress in your life. People who trigger an ending or spark a new beginning. People from overseas.

When? Saturdays. Late December through January.

Is This a Yes or a No? Yes. It's time for change.

KING OF WANDS

Advice for Right Now/Today You've come a long way, and you've come to understand a great deal about your authentic passions, interests, and motivations. You know what makes you tick. So why deviate from that? Don't shape-shift into other people's desires for or expectations of you; be your glorious and unique self through and through. It's time to lead others rather than be led. It's time to be in full control of your life. It's time to manifest your power at its full potential.

Affirmation I am designing every aspect of the life I am excited to lead.

A Reassurance Experience takes time to earn. Wisdom is hard-won. Self-awareness comes with time, struggle, reflection, and wrong turns. Don't worry about who you used to be or what you used to do. All those old versions of you got you to this place now, with all your hard-won experience and wisdom. No regrets.

Life Lesson It can take a while to grow into your own skin and feel comfortable in it. We all try out different styles, facades, pathways, and roles. It's the only way to truly find out who you are. Now that you know, be proud of that person.

A Challenge How authentically are you living your life? Ask yourself if you are working on and investing time in self-improvement, fulfilling your potential, living well, seeing the world and learning more, being entertained, and enjoying good friends. If not, time for change.

Do This Realign your activities, roles, and to-do list with your true desires and ambitions. Seek leadership roles. Advise others. Be in the midst of things.

Don't Do This Dwell in regret for time wasted or spent poorly, missed opportunities, and missteps.

Who? Fire signs (Aries, Leo, and Sagittarius). Possibly an older man who is exciting, inspiring, and full of ambition and wisdom.

When? A time span of weeks. Spring. Possibly April, August, or December.

Is This a Yes or a No? Yes. Take a chance because everything is a risk anyway.

QUEEN OF WANDS

Advice for Right Now/Today This is a powerful day, a shift in terms of your appetite for, and degree of, control over and direction in your life. You realize you need to stand up and make things happen for yourself. You understand your passions need pursuit and attraction; they're not just going to fall into your lap. Horizons are broadening, options are opening up, and you see how you're becoming the master of your own destiny at last.

Affirmation I am taking control of my life today.

A Reassurance Adventures require preparation and planning. Even fun and joyful holidays or trips necessitate some research and someone to be in charge, to make the decisions and call the shots. This is you. This is adulting. You are doing what needs to be done.

Life Lesson We all play various secret and subconscious roles in relation to others in our lives. To some we're a parent figure, to others a child. The Queen of Wands shows that you're becoming the adult, the parent, the voice of authority. This is you stepping into your own power.

A Challenge What do you truly want to book, plan, create, propose, pitch, or make a reality? Is anyone else going to do this for you? No. So what's stopping you making it happen for yourself?

Do This Book a trip or holiday. Start the process of moving home. Apply for a dream role. Start a course. Get creative. Exercise and begin a new positive healthy regime. Seek a promotion. Pitch an idea.

Don't Do This Stay in familiar waters, treading water, waiting to see what others do first.

Who? Fire signs (Aries, Leo, and Sagittarius). Possibly an older woman who is dynamic, direct, and full of life.

When? A time span of weeks. Spring. Possibly April, August, or December.

Is This a Yes or a No? Yes. Be bold.

KNIGHT OF WANDS

Advice for Right Now/Today Some days are quiet and peaceful; some are dull and boring. That won't be today! The Knight of Wands is a passionate, headstrong character who follows his heart wherever it takes him, and to heck with the consequences. Sometimes this works, sometimes it doesn't, but when you're in the throes of a passionate urge, desire, or idea, you don't really care about tomorrow. It's all about what you want today. Go for it.

Affirmation I commit to living my life with passion, joy, and excitement.

A Reassurance Life's for living, right? You'll be dead a long time, so ignore what looks sensible on paper and embrace following your heart's desires and having adventures. Be safe, be yourself, and be kind . . . but be fun!

Life Lesson The worst that can happen is that you'll make a mistake you can learn from. Don't avoid doing things you feel truly animated about for fear of what others think or what might happen in a worst-case scenario.

A Challenge Make today bolder, brighter, and more fun. Inject excitement and thrills into your schedule. If that is totally impossible today, then plan and book something to look forward to in the week ahead.

Do This Go out and socialize. Be around uplifting and upbeat people. Go to a theme park or a place with exciting activities to do. Take a chance.

Don't Do This Talk yourself out of your passions and ideas because of fear or worry.

Who? Fire signs (Aries, Leo, and Sagittarius). People who are motivated, energetic, full of life, and great to be around.

When? A time span of weeks. Spring. Possibly April, August, or December.

Is This a Yes or a No? Yes. Go for it.

PAGE OF WANDS

Advice for Right Now/Today A youthful, carefree, experimental energy settles over you today—enjoy it and go with it! Release all pressure to do things perfectly. Just enjoy whatever it is you're doing and be grateful for the results—or lessons, if it goes awry a little. Have a go; throw your hat in the ring. Follow interests and pursuits that excite you. When you're young and carefree, you behave like you're bulletproof. It doesn't last forever, so enjoy the feeling while you have it.

Affirmation I am full of vitality, energy, and passion.

A Reassurance They always say "old too soon and smart too late," and it's true. But today you're getting a blast of that pure, unadulterated, youthful vigor, so use it well and believe that anything is possible. Live like you're young and riding on a wave of good fortune.

Life Lesson Youthfulness is as much a mindset as it is a literal number. Think young, be open-minded, pursue passions, and look for fun. Be young again.

A Challenge What would you do if you were invincible, couldn't fail, and felt full of confidence? Pick a project, task, or idea. Make today the day to go at it full force, with 100 percent belief and no fear of what may come.

Do This Live large. Have fun. Experiment. Have a go and try it. Take off all the pressure.

Don't Do This Let perfectionism or fear paralyze your ability to take action or join in.

Who? Fire signs (Aries, Leo, and Sagittarius). People who are full of life, creativity, and energy.

When? A time span of weeks. Spring. Possibly April, August, or December.

Is This a Yes or a No? Yes. What the heck, do it.

ACE OF WANDS

Advice for Right Now/Today You are ready to start something new, something inspiring, or something that fills you with optimism and enthusiasm and is authentically suited to you and your interests and talents. It could be a new hobby, course, class, creative project, travel idea or journey, role, lifestyle or well-being regime, friendship, mentorship, or even just a book or show. You are inviting, creating, and welcoming a new stimulus into your world today. It feels great!

Affirmation I am the creator of my reality.

A Reassurance Environment is everything—what we surround ourselves with, where we go, and what we feed to our brain. Create a positive, inspiring, uplifting environment for yourself and you will lead a happy life.

Life Lesson Creativity is one of humankind's superpowers; it's what has separated us from other life on Earth. Use this power and create content, activity, and a stimulus in your life that excites you.

A Challenge Know that by the end of today, you will have activated something new to do. Whether this is related to education, travel, creativity, lifestyle, or connection is up to you. But resolve to embrace a new addition today.

Do This Research new hobbies and activities. Look at local classes, workshops, and lectures available to you. Go to the library. Seek a mentor. Take one step toward better health.

Don't Do This Default back to what you already do and know instead of something new.

Who? Fire signs (Aries, Leo, and Sagittarius). People who can inspire and encourage you to make a fresh start on something fulfilling.

When? Up to a one-week time span. Spring. Possibly April, August, or December.

Is This a Yes or a No? Yes. Go for it.

TWO OF WANDS

Advice for Right Now/Today You might feel you have got a lot going on right now but it's all a little half-baked. Projects that began with gusto have hit a snag, ideas remain vague, relationships are blowing hot and cold, or tasks look onerous and remain unfinished. It's a day to clear house! Re-prioritize and refocus. A lot of what you've started can be abandoned; it's not worth it anymore. That's okay. Get rid of the dead wood and establish what's important from what remains.

Affirmation I put first things first.

A Reassurance Don't prioritize what's already on your schedule; reschedule according to your priorities. To do that, you must first refocus on what your priorities are. That's all you really need to do today. Streamline and refocus.

Life Lesson You can't be anything you want, but you can be everything you already are. Refocus your goals around what works for you naturally, what enhances your interests and skills, and where you feel at home and at ease.

A Challenge Commit to having a much shorter to-do list by the end of today than you've got right now. Make it a to-do list that is ruthlessly focused on the big rocks in your life (which means knowing exactly what they are).

Do This Streamline. Audit where your time and energy are going. Make a five-year plan. Revisit your goals. End, delay, or delegate stuff that isn't urgent, important, or uniquely you. Get clarity on your tasks.

Don't Do This Lean into the feelings of confusion or overwhelm. Continue to spread yourself too thinly.

Who? Fire signs (Aries, Leo, and Sagittarius). People who might tempt you into roles, tasks, or projects that don't serve your ultimate goals.

When? Up to a two-week time span. Spring. Possibly April, August, or December.

Is This a Yes or a No? No. You are at risk of being distracted from your true ambitions.

THREE OF WANDS

Advice for Right Now/Today Manifest! Bring an idea to fruition. Activate a creative vision. Start an enterprise that is purely a product of your imagination. Today, there is magic swirling all around you, so go out on a limb! Opportunities, invitations, and openings will magically appear before you. If you step forward into the ether, a path will unexpectedly rise to meet your tread. It might look like luck to others, but you know what you're doing.

Affirmation I am ready to create the life of my dreams.

A Reassurance Luck happens when intent and preparation meet opportunity, and today is that day.

Life Lesson You make your own luck in this life.

A Challenge Wear a super-intense and alert lens today. Be receptive to and proactive about spotting openings and opportunities. Even if they seem like a wild card, or maybe even unrelated to your cause, have a go, throw your hat in, join in, and talk to them. Things will unfold unexpectedly today.

Do This Take a chance. Apply. Create something. Start something. Put yourself forward. Have a go. Trial a new method or process.

Don't Do This Wait and see what happens. Do nothing.

Who? Fire signs (Aries, Leo, and Sagittarius). People who have got amazing opportunities for you (but they won't hang around for long, so act fast).

When? Up to a three-week time span. Spring. Possibly April, August, or December.

Is This a Yes or a No? Yes. Take a chance.

FOUR OF WANDS

Advice for Right Now/Today You are on a roll and in the flow. Things have been going well, and you're ready to build on your successes. Make your plans bigger and bolder with the Universe backing you up. This is a great time to think about expanding your horizons—moving home or even to a new location/country for work or studies. This card is about going global! The sky's the limit for you right now, so dream big and build on what you've already achieved.

Affirmation I am talented, skillful, creative, and unique.

A Reassurance Sometimes everything just falls into place, the stars align, and good fortune rains down on us. Enjoy these phases; don't overthink them or self-sabotage or worry about things going wrong. Play while you're winning and bank some more wins!

Life Lesson Don't wait for opportunity; create it.

A Challenge Look at where you have enjoyed the most successes, rewards, recognition, or praise. Ask for feedback if you feel unsure. Zoom in on your strengths and the field of play they open up to you. Look at what the next level, step, or goal could be for you. Consider location as a means of opening up new opportunities.

Do This Apply for a dream role or course. Look at dream locations you'd like to live, study, or work in. Get feedback on what you're uniquely good at. Zoom in on what you enjoy and explore doing more there.

Don't Do This Continue to pursue a career or pathway that isn't really you or doesn't play to your natural strengths and interests.

Who? Fire signs (Aries, Leo, and Sagittarius). People who are encouraging and inspiring and want you to fulfill your maximum potential.

When? Up to a four-week time span. Spring. Possibly April, August, or December.

Is This a Yes or a No? Yes. Dream big and aim high.

FIVE OF WANDS

Advice for Right Now/Today This card represents the first agents of change in your life, inevitably resulting in conflict, discomfort, or pressure. You are tussling with someone or something, and maybe tempers have frayed and strong words have been said. Don't add fuel to the fires of disagreement. Go within and find their triggers, drivers, and root causes. Work on what it all means. Stop the fighting, make peace, and look for a different way forward that answers these tensions and evokes change.

Affirmation I am going to transform this moment and remove all limitations.

A Reassurance Most people don't enjoy or seek conflict or squabbles, even though most people go through them. If you offer a compromise, solution, or even just a truce, they're likely to seize it with gusto. Let things simmer down, and meanwhile you can analyze what has led to this.

Life Lesson Learning to actually value conflict might be your life lesson today. Conflict can highlight problems and provide motivation for change. It can be viewed as a precursor to progress.

A Challenge Draw the drama to a close today by any means necessary. End the feuding, squabbling, bickering, and backbiting. Buy yourself space and room to think.

Do This Ask for a time-out. Withdraw. Atone for your role in things. Genuinely seek your opponent's point of view and listen well, try to understand the other side of the coin. Look for insights as to what this means for you and how you can make a change to address it.

Don't Do This Carry on adding to the drama and noise.

Who? Fire signs (Aries, Leo, and Sagittarius). People you may need to make peace with.

When? Up to a five-week time span. Spring. Possibly April, August, or December.

Is This a Yes or a No? No. It's likely to create strife and tension.

SIX OF WANDS

Advice for Right Now/Today You're on a roll. You're riding the waves of success, victory, and progress, and there's more to come. Today is a day of optimism, hope, activity, and rewards. You deserve this. You have worked for it, so enjoy it! And ready yourself to build on it for the future. Lean into your gifts, talents, strengths, and opportunities. Celebrate yourself and others. Show gratitude. Tell other people how much you appreciate them. Share the joy!

Affirmation I am going to make today count.

A Reassurance When the going is good, keep going! Don't pause to wonder if or when this all might end. Don't undermine your own confidence or enthusiasm. Use the rewards you're reaping today to plant even more seeds for success down the line.

Life Lesson Many people believe, and think they have proven, that the key trait that differentiates successful people from others is their degree of optimism— looking on the bright side, seeing the positives. Put this to the test today.

A Challenge Identify what you're enjoying, succeeding in, or winning with right now that could be used to build something new in the future. Stretch, expand, develop, and embolden yourself based on your successes.

Do This Celebrate. Be grateful. Reward and appreciate those who've helped you. Notice what others have achieved recently and compliment them.

Don't Do This Worry about what might happen next instead of making something happen yourself.

Who? Fire signs (Aries, Leo, and Sagittarius). People you need to uplift, appreciate, and celebrate.

When? Up to a six-week time span. Spring. Possibly April, August, or December.

Is This a Yes or a No? Yes. This is going to be great.

SEVEN OF WANDS

Advice for Right Now/Today Stand up for yourself today. Showcase what you're good at, enjoy doing, and feel in flow with. In that space, you're unstoppable and unchallenged. Don't let self-doubt or imposter syndrome infect you today. Hold your head high, your chin up, and your chest out. The only person who can really do you in today is your own worst enemy . . . yourself. Keep the self-talk positive and upbeat. Be your best.

Affirmation I have the courage to express my unique self and strengths.

A Reassurance We all tend to downplay our own strengths or talents. Instead we compare our flaws or weaknesses to the highlights from someone else's reel. We focus on our own failings or lack. Why? Don't do this to yourself today. You are admired and respected. Shine your brightest light.

Life Lesson The best comparisons you can draw in life are with your past self, to reflect on your own trajectory and growth (because you never truly know what someone else is going through, hiding, or projecting). If you must compare, then do so as an equal—not an inferior or a superior. Learn what you can from looking with a level gaze.

A Challenge See challenge, competition, and rivalry as opportunities or invitations to bring forth and showcase your best self, your strongest side, and your most resolute beliefs. Don't be afraid to put your head above the parapet today.

Do This Compete. Stand up for yourself and others. Be proud. Showcase a talent. Promote yourself and your ability. Pit yourself against a personal best or previous standard.

Don't Do This Dwell on your failings, flaws, or lack. Focus on where you feel weakest.

Who? Fire signs (Aries, Leo, and Sagittarius). People you can be inspired by.

When? Up to a seven-week time span. Spring. Possibly April, August, or December.

Is This a Yes or a No? Yes. This is a worthwhile challenge.

EIGHT OF WANDS

Advice for Right Now/Today Today, it's all about communication, networking, socializing, interacting, collaborating, talking, and connecting. Magic happens when your energy collides with another's and you can share and build something totally new together. You will find yourself right in the center of things today, and it feels empowering and enlivening.

Affirmation I am connected to the Universe and all that's going on in it.

A Reassurance We all go through phases during which we feel disconnected, lonely, or at a loss with others. It's normal, sometimes necessary, and actually sometimes welcome. But you can turn that around in a heartbeat. You know someone you can talk to, reach out to, or reconnect with. Start with one step and it will snowball.

Life Lesson In life, it's often about who you know more than what you know. Connect with others as much and as often as you can. It keeps you young and in opportunity's path.

A Challenge Look at your channels of communication, personal and professional, and give them a spruce-up. Update and refresh the ways you connect with others. Think about those you've lost touch with and miss, and reach out to them.

Do This Communicate broadly and widely. Be around others. Share information. Pay compliments. Ask for feedback. Apply. Join. Present. Pitch.

Don't Do This Stay in, stay home, close the door, shut the curtains, and be alone.

Who? Fire signs (Aries, Leo, and Sagittarius). People who have news, information, (good) gossip, invitations, or opportunities for you.

When? Up to an eight-week time span. Spring. Possibly April, August, or December.

Is This a Yes or a No? Yes. Throw your hat into the ring.

NINE OF WANDS

Advice for Right Now/Today Today is a day for tackling, overcoming, and blasting down barriers, obstacles, and pitfalls in your way. That includes things that have bothered you for a while or that you have dreaded facing. Don't worry! The cosmos is backing you today, and you will find magical powers, help, support, and guidance whenever you reach out or push outside a comfort zone. Growth stimulates more growth. On the other side of these obstacles lie smooth seas, so sail ahead!

Affirmation I am going to succeed and win today.

A Reassurance Most things seem worse from afar, as we dwell on them, than they actually are in real life. Action is often better than thought when you feel afraid. Action distracts and gets you moving, and it's certainly more productive than procrastination.

Life Lesson The hardest step is the first one. Push yourself into action today, force a move, and the momentum will start to flow with you. Prove you can do this (spoiler: you can).

A Challenge What do you wish you were waking up to find magically removed or addressed in your life? That is the thing you're going to tackle today. With confidence. You're unstoppable.

Do This Make a move. Try a different approach. Write down a list of possible solutions and work through them systematically. Ask for help. Seek advice.

Don't Do This Live in the horrible gray zone of dread and catastrophizing.

Who? Fire signs (Aries, Leo, and Sagittarius). People from whom you might need advice, help, or guidance today.

When? Up to a nine-week time span. Spring. Possibly April, August, or December.

Is This a Yes or a No? Yes. It will go better than you think.

TEN OF WANDS

Advice for Right Now/Today You're doing too much, you've taken too much on, and if you carry on like this, you will burn out. In that event, you won't be able to do any of your projects or priorities justice. This is unsustainable, and today is the day to address the balance and lighten the load. We all get into these pickles, because life is always busy, but the trick is to recognize the fatigue as a warning sign and do something proactive to change things.

Affirmation I have permission to release the unimportant, non-urgent, and unwelcome things on my plate.

A Reassurance You are only one day away from feeling much more capable, in control, and able to do what you need (and want) to do. Today is going to be a liberation from stuff that doesn't need doing under your watch. It's important to streamline right now.

Life Lesson You can't pour from an empty jug. Your energy, strength, resources, and attention span are not infinite. Sooner or later, you need to learn to focus on fewer, but more worthwhile, tasks and relationships.

A Challenge Imagine you were a consultant reviewing your schedule, to-do list, priorities, and needs. Is there time in the day for it all? Are there things that eat up a lot of time and energy but don't feel that important to you? Be objective, rational, and ruthless.

Do This Quit. Say no. Withdraw. Ask for an extension, pause, or total break.

Don't Do This Feel pressured or ashamed to admit you need a break and can't manage everything on your plate.

Who? Fire signs (Aries, Leo, and Sagittarius). People who might be putting you, even unconsciously, under pressure.

When? Up to a ten-week time span. Spring. Possibly April, August, or December.

Is This a Yes or a No? No. This will tip you over the edge.

KING OF COINS

Advice for Right Now/Today Be the very best version of yourself and think about your impact (direct and by example or one-step-removed) on others. You are a leader, in many respects, and an example. Amplify your strengths and acknowledge your weaknesses. Notice your fears and address them. Notice where others seek your company, advice, or help. Notice where you play a lead and lean into that role fully. Take responsibility.

Affirmation I matter to a lot of people.

A Reassurance We are all on the same journey, from vulnerable beginner to challenging student to skilled practitioner with increasing responsibilities and, finally, to master, with all the wisdom and experience that comes with that. Don't resist this journey. Embrace where you are. You are not alone in any of the stages. Seek guidance as needed.

Life Lesson You get the life you work for. Work hard, be good to others, and take responsibility.

A Challenge Compare yourself to the person you were five or ten years ago. Look at the growth, the transformations, the struggles, and the triumphs. Remind yourself you're evolving for the better all the time.

Do This Mentor. Coach. Advise. Support. Help. Give. Set an example. Focus on growth in your health, wealth, home, and work realms.

Don't Do This Blame others for where you are. Refuse to take ownership for your position or your future steps.

Who? Earth signs (Taurus, Virgo, and Capricorn). People who are inspiring examples to you and can provide great examples of strength, stoicism, and resilience.

When? Up to a one-year time span. Autumn. Possibly January, May, or September.

Is This a Yes or a No? Yes, especially if this helps out other people too.

QUEEN OF COINS

Advice for Right Now/Today Time to rise, to push outside of your comfort zone, and to reach for the next level. Lead. Set an example. You are emerging as a respected and trusted guide or lead in an area linked to health, wealth, home, or work. This responsibility includes taking extremely good care of yourself too.

Affirmation I have the power, will, and ability to be the leader I want to be.

A Reassurance Leadership is not about force or trickery. Power should be wielded with great care, for the good of others, not as a shield purely for yourself. You know this, and therefore you're wary of taking on powerful roles. Don't be. You are ready (as shown by your trepidation).

Life Lesson Step up and take hold of the wheel. We all have to take responsibility, and now is your time. You will learn as you go. Don't resist or feel afraid.

A Challenge Where, in your particular realm, are you ready for the next level? You will feel the answer acutely because it will be where you can just see what needs doing. Perhaps you feel frustrated at current processes. Perhaps you have passed all the tests and measures and you're ready to leverage those accomplishments in the real world. Perhaps you are restless. Find this place in your life and take action to move up.

Do This Apply for promotion. Accept the expansion or responsibility that is being offered or is available today. Practice self-care.

Don't Do This Yield to imposter syndrome and stay where it's safe and free of responsibility.

Who? Earth signs (Taurus, Virgo, and Capricorn). An older woman who is wise, shrewd, and worldly. Leaders. Mentors.

When? Up to a one-year time span. Autumn. Possibly January, May, or September.

Is This a Yes or a No? Yes, but make sure you've mitigated the risks.

KNIGHT OF COINS

Advice for Right Now/Today It's important, today of all days, to combine your conscientiousness with creativity. It's important to balance keeping your head down and focusing on your goal with looking up and around for new input and ideas. Don't close yourself off, but don't open up so wide you get distracted. Walk a balanced line between focus and awareness for optimum results in work, wealth, health, and home projects.

Affirmation I am fully present in whatever I am doing.

A Reassurance You've got this. You can do this. You have everything in place to succeed. What's required now is attention to detail and awareness of possible adjustments that would make the results even better.

Life Lesson We all need to learn a vital lesson in our life: how to master and manage our own efforts, focus, and attention. Self-discipline is a critical life skill; it is a make-or-break ability.

A Challenge Set timers or segment your day into chunks so you can both focus without distraction on complex or demanding tasks and seek inspiration, input, and feedback to make tweaks and changes as you go. Don't muddle your day up into one messy blob of activity—compartmentalize it.

Do This Focus. Concentrate. Plan an hour-by-hour schedule. Create windows of time to wander, ruminate, scroll, and discuss.

Don't Do This Lose yourself in distractions. Focus too hard for too long and burn out.

Who? Earth signs (Taurus, Virgo, and Capricorn). People who are committed to helping you fulfill your tasks and ambitions. Students. Teachers. Mentors.

When? A time span of at least a year. Autumn. Possibly January, May, or September.

Is This a Yes or a No? Yes, if you have answered all questions and doubts regarding this decision.

PAGE OF COINS

Advice for Right Now/Today We are all on a learning curve, we are all absorbing new information (formally or informally), and we are all perennial students. Notice this in yourself and your life today. Ask yourself if there are areas, skills, or pieces of information you'd like to educate yourself about specifically. Perhaps it's time to consciously decide what learning curves you're on.

Affirmation Education is the gateway to the future, and today I take charge of my education.

A Reassurance The more you learn, the less you realize you know. This is true no matter how old, experienced, or educated you are. Accept that you will never know enough and enjoy being open to learning more every day.

Life Lesson Live and learn. Perhaps the best way to approach life is as a series of tests and lessons from all directions that never end.

A Challenge Consider where you'd like to seek more education, be it for professional or personal reasons. Make a list. Research options. Activate your studies.

Do This Read a book. Listen to a podcast. Watch a documentary. Write down your key life lessons. Research courses or formal studies you'd like to do.

Don't Do This Think you know it all, because you don't.

Who? Earth signs (Taurus, Virgo, and Capricorn). People who have a relationship to education and learning.

When? A time span of at least one year. Autumn. Possibly January, May, or September.

Is This a Yes or a No? Yes, if this decision has the potential to teach you something.

ACE OF COINS

Advice for Right Now/Today This is a day to fix stuff relating to your material world, the places you inhabit every single day—that is, your own body, your home, your work, and your finances. Without a solid foundation here, you can feel unstable and out of control. Audit your health, wealth, work, and home. Are your accounts in order? Do you feel good? Do you enjoy your job? Is your home safe, maintained, and comfortable? Make a long-term plan of action to activate new beginnings and to tackle any and all flaws or longings in these areas.

Affirmation I am starting positive new habits and actions to make my world safe and secure.

A Reassurance You can start over anytime you like. You can undertake new beginnings and actions, making yourself feel more grounded and secure.

Life Lesson What worked before might not always work. Maintenance is vital and requires close observation of changing patterns and influences, as well as proactive responses to those shifts and needs. Be your own coach, personal trainer, manager, and financial guru.

A Challenge Look at the unmet—or poorly met—needs, desires, and frustrations in and around your material world, and make a top-three list of things to start doing to fix or fulfill them. Make these actions feasible, easy, and achievable *today* (even if each action is just a phone call or looking something up).

Do This Get your accounts in order. Start an investment or savings scheme. Join a gym or start an exercise regime. Eat healthy. Audit your career plans. Apply for a role.

Don't Do This Become overwhelmed by the scale of your ambitions or needs instead of breaking them down into feasible steps you can take each day that will add up to a much larger leap in time.

Who? Earth signs (Taurus, Virgo, and Capricorn). People who can help you clarify, commit to, and achieve a long-term goal.

When? Up to a one-year time span. Autumn. Possibly January, May, or September.

Is This a Yes or a No? Yes. It is time to activate a new beginning.

TWO OF COINS

Advice for Right Now/Today Abundance! Today is going to be super busy, but in a good way. Make sure you are fully fueled, rested, and ready to say yes to lots of new adventures. Gravitate to places you haven't visited before. Dive into new projects, roles, and relationships. Make your everyday life feel like a magical adventure by welcoming in new energy.

Affirmation I am looking for enlightenment and knowledge.

A Reassurance A busy, active life will probably have many compartments in it (work, family, creative projects, friends, relaxation, exercise, love life, travel ambitions, etc.). The more compartments you have open and active, the easier it is to bear loss or failure in a particular compartment because your energies are spread across more areas. In short, don't put all your eggs in one basket.

Life Lesson The more you do, the more you find you can do. Busy people get more done, so embrace being busy.

A Challenge Although it feels gimmicky, make today a day on which you say yes as often as possible. Be open-minded and open-hearted toward new people, places, invitations, demands, ideas, and activity.

Do This Say yes. That's it!

Don't Do This Be defensive, overprotective, brittle, or blocking. Feel like you have to retreat or cover up to keep your world intact instead of letting things flow to you because you are part of the world already.

Who? Earth signs (Taurus, Virgo, and Capricorn). People who have new news, ideas, or opportunities for you.

When? Up to a two-year time span. Autumn. Possibly January, May, or September.

Is This a Yes or a No? Yes. A resounding yes.

THREE OF COINS

Advice for Right Now/Today If energy can't be destroyed, but only transformed, then it follows that everything we invent or make is simply the rearrangement or transformation of existing energies and matter. You are a mixer! Notice the raw materials around you today (people, objects, ideas, channels, places, etc.). Consider how you can mix and match different things in order to create a new whole. Seek collaborators. Be a mad professor and invent something new from what is around you already.

Affirmation The inventor is already within me.

A Reassurance They say that nothing in the world is new. It's all been seen and done before; everything is a reinvention on an old theme. So use what you know. Rely on things you already understand, and just mix them with something else to update, recalibrate, improve, upgrade, or innovate.

Life Lesson Life is what you make it. We are all given a bag of tools, an hourglass, and a book of rules. Use them to your advantage.

A Challenge Look at where you want to see progress, improvement, or change in your life and examine the existing ingredients of that situation. How can you deconstruct and reassemble them to make a difference or to add something new to the mix?

Do This Brainstorm. Create. Invent. Seek input and collaboration. Work on improving a relationship, prospect, lead, project, area of your life, or personal goal. Experiment with new tech. Read a science book.

Don't Do This Shut down new thinking or input. Carry on doing what you always do and expecting it to yield different results. Feel like you have no power to effect change.

Who? Earth signs (Taurus, Virgo, and Capricorn). People who can work with you to bring about progress and advancement by doing something new with something old.

When? Up to a three-year time span. Autumn. Possibly January, May, or September.

Is This a Yes or a No? Yes, ideally if it benefits others as well as yourself.

FOUR OF COINS

Advice for Right Now/Today It's possible you feel stuck, bored, trapped, or constrained in a *Groundhog Day* scenario with this card's stagnant and same-old energy. We all get stuck in ruts, usually of our own making. Safety can lead to familiarity and, eventually, stagnation. So today is all about changing the record, shaking things up, starting afresh, being different, and taking a different approach.

Affirmation I change my life one step at time.

A Reassurance The best way to escape a rut is to just take one small step toward a new horizon. You'll reach a new place that will have different routes leading on from it, and in just three steps' time you might find yourself, naturally, in a whole new position. One step at a time.

Life Lesson Although change can be a bit scary or painful, nothing is as painful as being stuck someplace we don't want to be. Face the momentary and initial fear of making a change rather than the seeping and long-term pain of being stuck.

A Challenge Notice where you feel you are living with or experiencing the same-old routine or energy over and over, making you feel bored, frustrated, numb, fearful, or angry. Look at the triggers, habits, mental traps, and patterns around this area. Resolve to think of one small step you can take today to edge away from this rut. And do it.

Do This Walk a different way to your usual haunts. Call up someone you haven't spoken to in ages. Listen to a new podcast or radio station. Try a different food or drink. Ask someone a question you've never asked before. Mix up your schedule.

Don't Do This Carry on carrying on because you're fearful of what could change. The devil is not better because you know it!

Who? Earth signs (Taurus, Virgo, and Capricorn). People who are linked to your rut, be that in a positive way or a negative way. You might need to reconsider some connections.

When? Up to a four-year time span. Autumn. Possibly January, May, or September.

Is This a Yes or a No? Yes, if the answer is about making a change and doing something different.

FIVE OF COINS

Advice for Right Now/Today Sometimes when we experience sorrow, regret, or anxiety, the quickest way out is to focus on someone else and do a good turn. Doing good feels good and often results in gratitude and affection from the recipient of your goodwill. Process this echo and move on.

Affirmation I attract kind people, energy, and experiences into my life today.

A Reassurance We all have sorrow and regrets in our past. The longer you live, the more you will experience. Some call this baggage. That's perhaps a useful way to think of it because baggage can be donated, lost, packed away, recycled, or burnt! You can choose to shed your baggage. In fact, you should.

Life Lesson If you stare at the past, that is the direction you'll go in. Look ahead. Move ahead. Be hopeful.

A Challenge Acknowledge your emotions and then imagine them fading to tiny wisps of cloud in your mind's eye, so you can simply blow them away.

Do This Let go of and release old wounds, emotions, or recurring reenactments of past situations. Forgive yourself (and others). Do a good turn.

Don't Do This Wallow and fester in negative emotions linked to past events.

Who? Earth signs (Taurus, Virgo, and Capricorn). People who are linked to your past and perhaps caused you grief, sorrow, or guilt. Forgive them.

When? Up to a five-year time span. Autumn. Possibly January, May, or September.

Is This a Yes or a No? No. This course of action could lead to loss or regrets.

SIX OF COINS

Advice for Right Now/Today Today is all about sharing your resources, wealth, time, and energy for the good of others. Chalk up good karma points by doing kind deeds so you can (partly) recoup the positive energy, rewards, and bonuses down the line. Consider what actions you can take today to enhance and improve the status of your circle. Be a bright light.

Affirmation I am kind, and I attract good things because I do good things.

A Reassurance People don't always remember exactly what you said or did, but they will always remember how you made them feel. Be a beacon of kindness and generosity today and you can create, from very little, a deep well and halo of positive energy and reward.

Life Lesson Be the change you wish to see in the world. Want more fairness? Always be fair. Want more respect? Always be respectful. Want more kindness? Always be kind. When you are an example, you'll experience more of what you seek.

A Challenge Go out of your way today to be generous, charitable, supportive, kind, and caring. Emit good energy into the world.

Do This Pay compliments. Donate unwanted possessions. Surprise someone with a treat. Offer to help. Give to charity. Join a local group working on community improvements.

Don't Do This Focus on your own worries, needs, and lack.

Who? Earth signs (Taurus, Virgo, and Capricorn). People who are giving, kind, charitable, and always looking out for others. Potential great friends.

When? Up to a six-year time span. Autumn. Possibly January, May, or September.

Is This a Yes or a No? Yes, if this doesn't have a bad karma consequence.

SEVEN OF COINS

Advice for Right Now/Today Check in on the progress and status of your goals, ambitions, and dreams. Consider what you're actively working on. Are things turning out as you hoped? Are the rewards worth the sacrifices? Money can't buy happiness. Sometimes we spend all our time chasing something only to realize it was never going to return what we actually needed. Take a day to reflect. It's okay to make tweaks, change course, or flip your priorities.

Affirmation I choose my choices and have control over what I do.

A Reassurance You are never committed to carrying on with anything you don't wish to. There is always an exit. You have control; you can make new choices. You are free to redesign your course.

Life Lesson There is no magic pathway in our life. The path is made by walking, by taking steps and treading with commitment. Only when we're on a path can we truly judge if it's right for us. And we can always change course.

A Challenge Question whether what you're working on and investing in is bringing the returns and rewards you hoped for, needed, and expected. If not, work out what is missing. Make a change.

Do This Review and audit your investments, projects, career trajectory, hobbies, finances, and home goals. Seek professional counsel or input. Ask for feedback.

Don't Do This Carry on with the same old thing just because it's what you've always done or said you wanted.

Who? Earth signs (Taurus, Virgo, and Capricorn). People who are invested in or connected to a long-term project or ambition you've been working on.

When? Up to a seven-year time span. Autumn. Possibly January, May, or September.

Is This a Yes or a No? Yes, if this represents a change in direction based on current dissatisfaction.

EIGHT OF COINS

Advice for Right Now/Today Don't give up. Don't walk away just yet. One more day. You can't see it, but you are so very close to the breakthrough that will make this role, project, process, or relationship worthwhile. The rewards are definitely worth the effort. Today might be a grind, but get through it. Push on and press ahead; this is just the dark before the dawn.

Affirmation Today is today, not every day.

A Reassurance When we're in the thick of something and the going is hard, it's easy to get sucked into thinking things will be like this forever and it's hopeless or pointless to keep pushing on. You just can't see the overview, the helicopter vision, or the trajectory overall. You are making progress; stick with it.

Life Lesson Hard work beats talent when talent doesn't work hard. With genuine effort, persistence, and drive, you can accomplish almost anything.

A Challenge Don't get bogged down by everything you still need to do. Instead, zoom in on three things you can achieve today and focus on them. Break down your to-do list into bite-size chunks: a priority each for morning, afternoon, and the end of the day.

Do This Work hard and take a break. Then go again. Set a timer and do as much as you can before it rings. Organize a treat for later to reward yourself for getting through.

Don't Do This Feel overwhelmed. Feel hopeless. Go back to bed or hide away and stop trying.

Who? Earth signs (Taurus, Virgo, and Capricorn). People who inspire you to keep turning up and trying—maybe even a famous role model. Think of them today.

When? Up to an eight-year time span. Autumn. Possibly January, May, or September.

Is This a Yes or a No? Yes, if you are prepared to work hard to make it happen.

NINE OF COINS

Advice for Right Now/Today Enjoy everything you have and what you've worked for, earned, and deserve. Revel in your accomplishments and successes. Remind yourself of the story so far and what you've overcome already. Then get ready to build on those successes because they are a strong platform and you can get to the next level. Focus on health, wealth, work, and home. Make long-term goals based on your current position.

Affirmation I am building on my strengths and successes.

A Reassurance You aren't starting from scratch. You already have so much wisdom, experience, insight, and resilience. You are wiser than you think and more skilled in certain areas than you believe. Remember your successes. They are your platform to build on.

Life Lesson Life is better by design. When we drift along without much of a plan (as we sometimes do, sometimes for years), we might get lucky and land well, but we often end up going with someone else's flow, supporting their narrative, and sacrificing our own story.

A Challenge Project yourself ahead ten years. What is this person doing? This "future you" is based on your ideals now. This person is within reach. Start building up to that vision.

Do This Make a long-term plan for your health, wealth, home, and work. Meditate and visualize a future you. Review your investments. Get advice from older people living in the next life stage you're headed toward.

Don't Do This Drift. Wait and see. Stick your head in the sand about your future.

Who? Earth signs (Taurus, Virgo, and Capricorn). People who can bring wisdom and insight to help you build on your strengths and improve your life.

When? Up to a nine-year time span. Autumn. Possibly January, May, or September.

Is This a Yes or a No? Yes, particularly if this is going to lead to a steady, long-term, and sustainable shift in fortunes.

TEN OF COINS

Advice for Right Now/Today What does "happily ever after" mean to you personally, truly, deep down? Today could bring opportunities to plant seeds for a prosperous and fruitful future. Focus on your health, wealth, home, and work. Good things come to those who create them. Patience is key, but nothing will grow unless it is planted first.

Affirmation I know I can achieve anything I want in this lifetime.

A Reassurance Goals give you something to work toward, a general direction, and boundary to focus within, but there is no final destination because life is one big journey. So make sure you are enjoying the ride toward your goals. If you aren't, change them today!

Life Lesson Big trees grow from tiny acorns. Everything starts small, vulnerable, uncertain, and weak. But it has to start somewhere and then be nurtured, sustained, and supported to reach its full strength and potential. Your life goals follow this same life cycle.

A Challenge Serve your happily-ever-after dreams and ideals. Start long-term projects and investments with a ten-year time frame.

Do This Make sacrifices for the long-game goal. Start savings, investments, pensions, and mortgages. Join a gym or start a new healthy regime.

Don't Do This Focus on immediate and short-term gains or wins over and above long-term opportunities.

Who? Earth signs (Taurus, Virgo, and Capricorn). People who are well placed to help you make your happily-ever-after a reality.

When? Up to a ten-year time span. Autumn. Possibly January, May, or September.

Is This a Yes or a No? Yes, if it serves the long-term future.

KING OF SWORDS

Advice for Right Now/Today You are feeling bold, enlightened, sharp, and alert to opportunity today. You feel like manifesting. You are looking, clear-eyed, into your long-term future and prospects and projecting yourself ahead to taste the outcomes and rewards. Does this mean you're on the right path? Is now a good time to tweak your trajectory? Get a helicopter view of your path and assess it rationally.

Affirmation I am designing my future for a grateful "future me" today.

A Reassurance Many dreams and goals start in our heart with a spark of desire, and this fuels our motivation to get started. Then we need to hand over the project to our brain, to our inner King of Swords, to sense check, pressure test, research, and plan out the steps to manifesting it.

Life Lesson A goal without a plan is just a wish. Put meat on the bones of your dreams, fantasies, and ambitions today. If you don't, they'll just remain daydreams.

A Challenge Assess how many of your goals, ideals, or dreams have actual plans, timelines, and actions against them. How hard are you working for future you?

Do This Research. Plan. Strategize. Review. Assess.

Don't Do This Accept fate's hand. You are the master of your own destiny. Accept this role fully and commit to it.

Who? Air signs (Gemini, Libra, and Aquarius). People who can provide shrewd advice and help you see how to fulfill your potential.

When? A time span of months. Winter. Possibly February, June, or October.

Is This a Yes or a No? Yes, if it serves future you well.

QUEEN OF SWORDS

Advice for Right Now/Today You feel like taking control, heeding your head over your heart, and making decisions that make sense, are logical, and serve you best, regardless of what others might say or think about it. After all, you are responsible for your life; no one else is going to live it for you. This Queen is wise, shrewd, and knowing. She has been hurt and maybe sometimes feels like hurting others. Rise above those feelings and wield your power and wisdom judiciously. But wield it all the same, and for your own benefit.

Affirmation I am using my power to better my life.

A Reassurance Everyone has teeth and claws, and we all have to use them sometimes. Maybe it's to remind others that we're no pushover, maybe it's to demand our rights when they clash with another's desires, or maybe to forge ahead on our own steam. Bare your teeth and use your claws today.

Life Lesson Taking care of yourself means defending what you have and fighting for what you want sometimes. The prey has to overcome the predator if it wants to survive.

A Challenge Imagine a steely hearted, self-serving, and shrewd advisor were spending the day with you today. Their purpose is simply to point out the things you need to stop, start, or change in your life in order to better serve your goals and needs. Imagine their report at the end of the day; what would it say?

Do This Be logical and dispassionate. Audit and review your circumstances, roles, and relationships. Meditate. Tap into your own ideas and desires. Research and educate yourself on things you need to know.

Don't Do This Listen to counsel that sounds comforting, but you suspect, deep down, isn't entirely true or for your own benefit.

Who? Air signs (Gemini, Libra, and Aquarius). People who are in a position of strength and can help you fathom out home truths and insights.

When? A time span of months. Winter. Possibly February, June, or October.

Is This a Yes or a No? Yes, if you can manage this alone.

KNIGHT OF SWORDS

Advice for Right Now/Today Today you need to imagine that your Knight of Swords is walking beside you, protecting you from all dissent, conflict, and harm. He is your cosmic bodyguard who will provide the courage, self-confidence, and assertiveness you need today. It's the time to put your agenda front and center and push forward. Make demands. Be bossy, be bold, and be self-serving.

Affirmation I know what I want and I ask for it.

A Reassurance We all have to work hard to find our authentic assertive voice (often varying between aggressive and passive as we move along this learning curve). Be honest, know your rights, speak clearly, listen well, and be prepared to negotiate or compromise. Assertiveness is an art of persuasion.

Life Lesson If you do not stand up for yourself and pursue your own needs and desires, how will you ever get what you want, need, or deserve? Everyone is playing their own game (even the best and kindest of us). Put yourself first. No one else will.

A Challenge Do some homework on how to amplify and strengthen your assertive voice, practice successful negotiations, and handle difficult dialogues. Develop a strategy for tackling the situation and cherry pick pointers from your research that you feel will help you the most in your discussions. Put them into effect today by having one tough conversation or negotiation. Push yourself to initiate it and see it through.

Do This Express your feelings, thoughts, and desires. Activate a tough conversation. Control your emotions, especially anger. Read up on your rights and obligations. Read up on assertiveness.

Don't Do This Hope for rescue. Expect others to sort things out for you.

Who? Air signs (Gemini, Libra, and Aquarius). People you may need to work on and persuade to see your point of view. People you can negotiate with.

When? A time span of months. Winter. Possibly February, June, or October.

Is This a Yes or a No? Yes, if you are prepared to push for this and make it happen.

PAGE OF SWORDS

Advice for Right Now/Today You have been hedging your bets, playing both sides of the fence, or blowing hot and cold on a particular project, priority, person, place, or opportunity. The Page of Swords is a green light to just commit. If you continue to hedge, this opening could well close, leaving you out in the cold for no good reason. What are you afraid of? Face it and get past it.

Affirmation I pursue my goals and strive for excellence.

A Reassurance We all feel safer and more comfortable—and more entertained! —sitting in the stands and commentating on the action in play. But games cannot be won from the sidelines. You have to be on the field and playing. Come out of the stands and get on the field. There is nothing to lose and everything to gain.

Life Lesson Desire ignites motivation, but it's persistence, determination, and commitment that enable you to achieve the goals and successes you wish for.

A Challenge Look at where you've been inconsistent, unsure, on and off, or non-committal. Resolve to make a decision today about whether you're going to drop this altogether or commit. And if you're committing, make a plan (at least a month ahead) and make a start.

Do This Say yes. Confirm your interest. Make a plan of action. Join or sign up. Be positive.

Don't Do This Continue to hedge your bets and observe rather than act.

Who? Air signs (Gemini, Libra, and Aquarius). People who are difficult to pin down so you really aren't sure how they think or feel.

When? A time span of months. Winter. Possibly February, June, or October.

Is This a Yes or a No? Yes, if this represents a commitment to something you desire.

ACE OF SWORDS

Advice for Right Now/Today Everything starts in the mind, with a truth, insight, or idea. The Ace of Swords brings you such a gift today, and you can accelerate toward it by engaging fully with the truth in your life. Ask for feedback, start tough conversations, or admit something. Honesty is liberating. By speaking and seeking the truth today, you can release any mental or emotional burdens you've been carrying and gain new self-awareness. Always expect surprises when you start these conversations, and remember to listen well.

Affirmation I balance honesty with kindness.

A Reassurance People always fear truth, but the truth exists whether you acknowledge it or not and is influencing you already. Just because you haven't consciously said something out loud doesn't mean you're not already experiencing it. So just say it.

Life Lesson Until you know the truth, you're just dealing with vapor and illusion.

A Challenge Think about a conversation you've been putting off having. Think about what you want out of it. Prepare your words; consider their response. Think about a good environment for having this chat. Make it happen.

Do This Ask for feedback. Activate a difficult conversation. Acknowledge your faults or role in a bad situation. Reflect on conflict and see both sides.

Don't Do This Refuse to engage with reality. Continue to cover up or excuse troubling actions.

Who? Air signs (Gemini, Libra, and Aquarius). People whom you need to talk to honestly and openly.

When? Up to a one-month time span. Winter. Possibly February, June, or October.

Is This a Yes or a No? Yes, if it reflects the truth.

TWO OF SWORDS

Advice for Right Now/Today Today it's important to be impartial and weigh up the facts rationally. Keep a cool head. Make lists of pros and cons. Don't get lost in information or detail, but do seek to answer lingering questions so that you can make decisions based on your best knowledge and understanding. A decision that has hung over your head for a while needs to be made today. No more procrastination.

Affirmation I will consider all outcomes and make the right choice.

A Reassurance There are never any guarantees that your decisions are right (or wrong). Moving along and responding to circumstances is the best you can do. Procrastination achieves nothing. Action achieves momentum. Even if what you do turns out wrong, you can just make another choice.

Life Lesson Our time on Earth is limited, and your time is precious. Don't waste it overthinking something. Regrets come from not doing something, rather than failing; with failure, there is always a lesson to be learned and new options ahead.

A Challenge Resolve to make your toughest, most dreaded, most avoided decision today. Face into it. Ask for help if you need it. Do your research. Understand your options. Mitigate the risks. And decide.

Do This Use your head to make a decision and execute it—no regrets.

Don't Do This Procrastinate. Overthink. Dwell in doubts. Second-guess yourself. Backpedal.

Who? Air signs (Gemini, Libra, and Aquarius). People who are connected to a crossroads you are facing; perhaps they can help you.

When? Up to a two-month time span. Winter. Possibly February, June, or October.

Is This a Yes or a No? Yes or no. This is a choice *you* have to make; no one and no thing can make it for you.

THREE OF SWORDS

Advice for Right Now/Today Consider the theme of damage today. Are there causes you're leading or fighting for that may be counterproductive, causing more harm than good? Are you at the mercy of someone else's cruelty, betrayal, or dismissal? Are you still smarting from a wound inflicted by another? Reflect on this, spot the symptoms of pain and strife in your psyche, and surgically remove their sources from your life. Seek liberation from treachery and callousness, and try to move to a place of healing.

Affirmation I consciously let go, so I can heal and move on in peace.

A Reassurance We are all going to be subject to someone else's poor behavior at some point. We will also likely be the cause of pain for someone else. Relationships are messy. You don't have to keep taking it, though, nor do you have to carry on inflicting it when you're aware of what you're doing. Take control. Stop being in or near or around pain.

Life Lesson Many say you're the sum of the five people closest to you. Make sure you've got a strong five! Choose people who are positive, uplifting, supportive, and have your best interests at heart.

A Challenge Spot, stop, and prevent the sources of conflict, pain, wounding, turmoil, cruelty, or betrayal in your relationship landscape. Remove the flies in your ointment!

Do This Apologize. Withdraw from toxic people or situations. Block bad influences on social media. Express your feelings. Ask for the truth.

Don't Do This Hurt yourself in order to please another.

Who? Air signs (Gemini, Libra, and Aquarius). People who are either the cause, or recipient, of pain in your world.

When? Up to a three-month time span. Winter. Possibly February, June, or October.

Is This a Yes or a No? No. It will not end well.

FOUR OF SWORDS

Advice for Right Now/Today Whatever your battles, it's time to mount a strategic retreat, maybe even chalk up a loss, and make space and time to heal, recuperate, and recalibrate your flagging energies. Rest—deep rest—is vital. A time-out is needed. Take a mental, if not physical, vacation from your stresses and battles today. We are all at risk of burnout when we don't give ourselves room to process the action, absorb the changes, and restore our vitality.

Affirmation My peace is more important than anything right now.

A Reassurance We all need a time-out, a conscious break from the grind, or a mental vacation from our worries or cares. Most often, we keep on going until we burn out. Learn to recognize the red flags of fatigue or stress in yourself and act on them. Be your own doctor.

Life Lesson You can't pour from an empty jug. Time to replenish your reserves.

A Challenge Identify the things draining your energy most rapidly and negatively right now. Do whatever you can to either remove them from your life or vastly diminish their impact on you.

Do This Make today all about deep rest. Get a massage. Go to bed very early. Book a vacation. Take the day off.

Don't Do This Ignore signs of strain and carry on at this pace. You will burn out.

Who? Air signs (Gemini, Libra, and Aquarius). People who are pushing you to some kind of limit.

When? Up to a four-month time span. Winter. Possibly February, June, or October.

Is This a Yes or a No? No. Now is not the right time for major decisions or to take on anything new.

FIVE OF SWORDS

Advice for Right Now/Today Today is the day to draw any and all skirmishes, tensions, battles, or conflicts in your life to a total close, a pause, a truce, or a place of healing and release. Stop fighting. What's the point? You aren't making things better. You are planting deeper seeds of resentment, anger, and recrimination. We all think we can win these battles, but anything causing anguish or rage rarely yields a winner in the long run. People don't forget.

Affirmation I am at peace with my ego and free from arguments.

A Reassurance Conflict with other people is unavoidable and we all go through it. There is, in truth, no winning outcome (even if you think you've won). People store resentments and anger for years, poisoning themselves and others. Bad vibes don't make anyone happy. So don't draw out your conflicts. Acknowledge they happened, find a root cause, kill your ego, and seek a way out.

Life Lesson Arguing is not communication. It's noise. It deflects and distracts from what really needs to be said, understood, or absorbed.

A Challenge Look at your battles from the other person's point of view. Find their reasoning for their position or stance. Understand it.

Do This Forgive and forget. Suggest a compromise. Apologize. End a relationship that is toxic. Seek mediation, negotiation, or even counseling. Call a truce. Prioritize peace.

Don't Do This Add fuel to the fire.

Who? Air signs (Gemini, Libra, and Aquarius). People who are at odds with you right now.

When? Up to a five-month time span. Winter. Possibly February, June, or October.

Is This a Yes or a No? No. What you're doing could create conflict and turmoil.

SIX OF SWORDS

Advice for Right Now/Today You have reached a crossroads and you're ready to move on from something, someone, or someplace. It's not sad or difficult because this is a natural conclusion, something that has run its course, or an ending that has been on the cards for a while. Be gracious and appreciative, but say goodbye to things that no longer warrant a place in your future. Make this bold leap in good spirits, knowing you're simply following the flow of energies in your landscape.

Affirmation I am moving on. I am releasing. I am evolving.

A Reassurance Everything ends. Everything has its time in the sun, its season in the shadow, and its final ebb. Don't cling to what's passing; in doing so, you're preventing new, necessary energy from flowing your way. Make space.

Life Lesson Change is the only constant in this life. Learn to be friends with it—sometimes seeking it, sometimes initiating it, and sometimes being led by it.

A Challenge Look at what is coming to a natural conclusion or to fruition in your realm. Accept this as inevitable, normal, and actually welcome because it frees you up to pursue something new and challenging.

Do This Quit. Leave. Say goodbye. Move. Relocate. Travel. Research your future options. Press ahead. Release the past. Grow.

Don't Do This Cling to things because they're familiar and safe.

Who? Air signs (Gemini, Libra, and Aquarius). People who are new in town or on the scene. Travelers. People you may be ready to move on from.

When? Up to a six-month time span. Winter. Possibly February, June, or October.

Is This a Yes or a No? Yes, especially if you are moving on to something new.

SEVEN OF SWORDS

Advice for Right Now/Today Keep your guard up today and listen to your gut in regard to the wholesomeness or good intentions of people, situations, and places you've invested in. There might be treachery or sabotage afoot. You might be close to someone who does not have your best interests at heart. Be careful, cautious, and protective of yourself. Withdraw from those you don't trust. Block the gossips. Sidestep the bullies. Be stony-faced around the saboteurs. You know who they are.

Affirmation I bestow my trust wisely and shrewdly.

A Reassurance You can't always judge others by your own high standards. People are strange, and they are driven by private motivations and agendas. When your instincts are aroused, trust that inner sat nav and retreat. This is a powerful life lesson.

Life Lesson Toxic people pollute the air around them; they seep into the pores of everything they touch. You can't change these folks. They are on their own strange journey that has deep roots and a long tail of woe behind it. The only way through is out. Learn to spot the signs of toxicity, protect yourself, and withdraw.

A Challenge Use today to tune in to your gut feelings about people and situations. Truly notice how your body responds to situations—whether you feel comfortable and open or wary and nervous. Use this information.

Do This Keep your cards close to your chest. Pause and wait to see what happens. Let others speak first. Withdraw from toxicity. End painful friendships.

Don't Do This Override your instincts and carry on confiding in or trusting someone who, deep down, you doubt is really on your side.

Who? Air signs (Gemini, Libra, and Aquarius). People who have the potential to hurt you for their own gains.

When? Up to a seven-month time span. Winter. Possibly February, June, or October.

Is This a Yes or a No? No. Be cautious and prudent.

EIGHT OF SWORDS

Advice for Right Now/Today Today is the day to break free of any and all mental prisons that have held you back or down. Seek genuine newness, innovation, invention, and different ways of approaching age-old issues or situations in your life. Imagine yourself as an innovator, as playing your games and roles on the cutting edge of fresh ideas and advancements. Sweep away old thinking. Stop projecting your fears outward or repeating bad habits. Be new, be different . . . and get different results.

Affirmation I amplify my ingenuity in everything I do today.

A Reassurance The older we get, the more resistant we become (even subconsciously) to new ideas. Despite thinking we want novelty and newness, we can find them unsettling or unnerving. We all feel this way, and it's okay. Consciously push out of this comfort zone and embrace the new; it will keep you youthful and let you in on secrets and tricks you can use.

Life Lesson If you've got enough nerve, you can achieve almost anything. You don't know what you're capable of until you push out of your comfort zone and try. Staying in familiar territory will see you circling the same results.

A Challenge Challenge yourself to be open, all day long, to brand-new ideas, voices, ideas, theories, methods, products, gadgets, and technology. Seek to do everything in a different way.

Do This Embrace a new technology. Talk to someone you usually wouldn't. Listen to a new radio station or podcast. Buy a book. Brainstorm. Invent.

Don't Do This Bed down in the same routines, approaches, beliefs, and methods. Be your own worst enemy. Be a drudge, a Luddite, or a doubter.

Who? Air signs (Gemini, Libra, and Aquarius). People who can present you with a totally new way of approaching something.

When? Up to an eight-month time span. Winter. Possibly February, June, or October.

Is This a Yes or a No? Yes, if this represents fresh thinking or action.

NINE OF SWORDS

Advice for Right Now/Today This card is like the therapist of the tarot, urging you to dive into your subconscious and draw forth the unspoken fears, concerns, anxieties, and unanswered questions that swirl chaotically around your mind at 4:00 in the morning. It's interested in the things that keep you awake—the things you keep private and bottled up. Today is the day to expel them because they are weighing you down. Once they are vented in the cold light of day, you can assess their true nature and value. Are they even worth addressing?

Affirmation I am safe. I am brave. I am in control.

A Reassurance We all experience spiraling—repetitive, negative thoughts and emotions (particularly in the waking hours). Most of this is vapor, hauntings, and excess mental energy burning up. The trick is always to release it. Name the feeling, look at it dispassionately, and figure out if action is needed or not (often it is not). Once you have exorcised the unnecessary and created an action plan for the valid, you will rest easier.

Life Lesson You can't run from yourself. Turn and face your shadows and fears. Talk to them. They are trying (often misguidedly) to protect you.

A Challenge Write down your most private, strongest, or most often recurring fears and worries. Speak their names and sources out loud to a mirror. Call a friend or family member and talk about them. If these feelings weigh too heavily, make a doctor's appointment.

Do This Journal. Mirror talk. Confide in someone. Make an appointment. Review your mental health. Purge your secret fears.

Don't Do This Bottle everything up and hope it will all just stop or go away.

Who? Air signs (Gemini, Libra, and Aquarius). People who are well placed to support you in untangling your anxieties and making a plan to tackle them.

When? Up to a nine-month time span. Winter. Possibly February, June, or October.

Is This a Yes or a No? No. This would create unwanted stress and turmoil.

TEN OF SWORDS

Advice for Right Now/Today Today is all about freedom, release, and total permission to leave behind anything negative, toxic, heavy, or troubling in your life. Whether it's work, family, friends, love, obligations, ambitions, or tasks, if it's ruining your peace of mind and hasn't shown signs of improvement (be honest), then it's time to depart from it and move on to better things. Today is about release. You need to clear out.

Affirmation Every ending is an opportunity to welcome something new.

A Reassurance We all have our own reasons for sticking with something, someplace, or someone that doesn't serve us well. We often fear the alternative (better the devil you know). But there comes a time when you have to protect yourself, draw a line, and take that leap into the unknown. Nothing is worse than being stuck in a situation that drags you down. It won't improve, and you will get weaker. Leave now.

Life Lesson Avoiding or leaving behind something toxic and draining isn't weakness; it's wisdom. Live to fight another day, a new battle, or a different story. This one is over.

A Challenge Ask yourself where you have been struggling the most in your life, for a long time now, and where it's starting to feel very negative and even hopeless. Pinpoint the investments you are making that are not paying you back.

Do This Quit. Leave. Move on. Withdraw. Block. Avoid. Separate.

Don't Do This Sacrifice your own ambitions, desires, and peace of mind to keep the peace elsewhere.

Who? Air signs (Gemini, Libra, and Aquarius). People who are no longer deserving of a place in your life.

When? Up to a ten-month time span. Winter. Possibly February, June, or October.

Is This a Yes or a No? No. This option will not bring you happiness.

KING OF CUPS

Advice for Right Now/Today Emotional intelligence is one of life's most sought-after and hard-won skills. It gives you the ability to both manage your own emotions and understand the emotions of those around you. There are five key elements: self-awareness, self-regulation, motivation, empathy, and social skills. The wise and compassionate King of Cups is telling you that today is the day to practice and wield your emotional intelligence for the benefit of yourself and those you love and like.

Affirmation I am compassionate toward and understanding of the people in my life.

A Reassurance Good people do bad things. Bad people do good things. Every saint has a past, and every sinner has a future. People are complicated, multi-layered, and all capable of both greatness and terribleness. That includes you. Seek to understand rather than judge.

Life Lesson Understanding others is one of our most potent abilities, but it requires us to be vulnerable too. To truly understand someone else, you must feel their emotions and perspective within yourself someplace. You must open up to others' ideas, feelings, and points of view and recognize parallels in your own experience.

A Challenge Cultivate pauses and room in your schedule to reflect and think today. Don't knee-jerk react to anything that happens or that you hear or see. Take a breath and think about the situation from another's perspective. Seek to understand all that is happening around you before you act.

Do This Practice observing how you feel. Question your own opinions. Take responsibility for your feelings. Take time to celebrate the positive, but don't ignore the negative.

Don't Do This Judge other people harshly.

Who? Water signs (Pisces, Cancer, and Scorpio). Possibly an older man. People who are wise, understanding, uplifting, and kind.

When? A time span of days. Summer. Possibly March, July, or November.

Is This a Yes or a No? Yes, if it doesn't harm another.

QUEEN OF CUPS

Advice for Right Now/Today Self-care is your theme song and priority today. And that doesn't mean staying in bed, eating chocolates, and taking long baths. Yes, there's an element of deep rest, pampering, and nurturing, but first you have to earn it! Then you will enjoy it all the more and feel rewarded.

Affirmation I make a difference to the world. I am valued.

A Reassurance Self-care is not self-centered or frivolous. It is simply good stewardship of your most precious asset: your health and well-being. You have to take care of you.

Life Lesson Almost everything will work again if you unplug it for a few minutes, and that includes you.

A Challenge Make the first part of today all about either facing a challenge or helping another in a selfless way. Be a presence for good and kindness today. Prove your own strength and value. And then reward yourself.

Do This Give generously and thoughtfully to others who need help. Tackle or overcome a challenge or issue in your life. Put aside time throughout the day for treats, reflection, and rest. Make your evening all about nurturing, positive, restoring rituals and practices.

Don't Do This Be overindulgent. Be self-pitying. Be lazy.

Who? Water signs (Pisces, Cancer, and Scorpio). Possibly an older, mother-like figure. People who want the very best for you.

When? A time span of days. Summer. Possibly March, July, or November.

Is This a Yes or a No? Yes. Do what is right for you.

KNIGHT OF CUPS

Advice for Right Now/Today Make your life feel like a fairy tale today, whether that means immersing yourself in your favorite books or films, spending time in magical places, enacting a heroic quest, or playing the romantic lead in your own love story. This is a day you can let yourself be totally carried away by fantasy, imaginative play, idealized daydreams, and escapism. See the magic in the everyday.

Affirmation I see magic all around me.

A Reassurance Life can be hard, gritty, testing, and grinding—no doubt about that. But we can create oases for ourselves where life is easier, freer, laced with magic, fueled by the fantastical and supernatural, blessed with romance, and enchanted by spells. Find ways to insert these pockets into your daily life and no one can take them away from you. This card is a reminder that life can be magical too.

Life Lesson Roald Dahl said that "those who don't believe in magic will never find it." Give magic a chance and, for today, believe in it. See what happens.

A Challenge Be a source of magic and romance today. Conjure up absorbing rituals, role-playing games, intriguing pastimes, and extraordinary experiences for yourself throughout the day.

Do This Gift someone a horoscope, crystal, or esoteric gift. Surprise your favorite person with an imaginative outing. Have a reading. Write your life story as a fairy tale. Immerse yourself in fantasy content.

Don't Do This Believe that childhood pursuits are only for children. Be hard and cynical.

Who? Water signs (Pisces, Cancer, and Scorpio). People with whom you can fall in love or become best friends.

When? A time span of days. Summer. Possibly March, July, or November.

Is This a Yes or a No? Yes. Live the dream.

PAGE OF CUPS

Advice for Right Now/Today A creative, wide-eyed, wholesome, dare I say slightly naïve (in a nice way) mood takes you by the hand today and leads you into new and interesting spaces, places, and opportunities. You will experience genuine wonderment at the world, like you're seeing everything with new eyes. Maybe you are. But keep your wits about you. Let that inner child out to play, but make sure your adult self is keeping a watch over them.

Affirmation I am open to all new experiences and ideas.

A Reassurance There's a necessary balance to be found between cynicism and naïveté. When we're cynical, we become dogmatic and stuck in a defensive position. When we're naïve, we're susceptible to others' cynicism and scheming. It's important to temper both extremes. See with wide-open, childlike eyes, but act with shrewd, adult-weathered controls and measures.

Life Lesson Love all, but trust only a few.

A Challenge Have an internal conversation with your inner child. What is exciting, interesting, or intriguing them right now? Where do they most want to play? Promise to devote time today to fulfilling that wish. As an adult, you can do that now, right? That's a gift right there.

Do This Play. Be nostalgic. Get creative. Explore a quirky venue. Listen to totally new ideas or theories about life.

Don't Do This Take everything at absolute face value instead of exercising some discernment.

Who? Water signs (Pisces, Cancer, and Scorpio). People who are creative, full of novel or inventive ideas, and love philosophizing.

When? A time span of days. Summer. Possibly March, July, or November.

Is This a Yes or a No? Yes, but be careful.

ACE OF CUPS

Advice for Right Now/Today Today will bring a magical, life-affirming new beginning to you. This is something pure, emotional, transformational, and powerful. Love, fertility, and creativity are also strongly indicated when this card arises. New relationships, especially romances or deep friendships, are likely. If you're thinking of starting or growing your family, then today's a good day to start trying! If you're brewing a new creative idea, today will provide a window of opportunity to breathe life into it.

Affirmation My heart is open to attracting unlimited abundance in my life.

A Reassurance Nothing is guaranteed, but if you never try, you will never know. Be led by hope (rather than by fear, distrust, or cynicism) today. Be wholesome, openhearted, loving, and kind. Smile and the world will smile right back.

Life Lesson Your powers of attraction are real. You attract what you emit and what you focus on. Put this to the test today by visualizing and focusing on what newness you wish to bring into your wonderful world.

A Challenge Read about and practice the Law of Attraction today, especially focused around love, fertility, and creativity (whichever is most relevant to you right now). Basically, whatever you pay attention to will come to you.

Do This Visualize. Manifest. Use the Law of Attraction. Invest in a potential or new relationship. Activate your creativity. Make a baby. Get a pet.

Don't Do This Block or resist new people, ideas, or opportunities because you can't guarantee the outcome.

Who? Water signs (Pisces, Cancer, and Scorpio). People who are potential new friends or lovers.

When? Up to a one-day time span. Summer. Possibly March, July, or November.

Is This a Yes or a No? Yes. This is going to be magical.

TWO OF CUPS

Advice for Right Now/Today Think about your hoped for, blossoming, new, and potential relationships. Who's in the landscape? What's happening with them? Relationships should ideally start off on the right foot, from a good place, and with positive intentions and behaviors. You should feel good about new people in your life. This card is a prompt to invest in, prioritize, and make progress on your most rewarding, romantic, and healthy relationships today.

Affirmation I attract trusting and loving relationships.

A Reassurance Healthy, positive relationships require two people who share a commitment to working on it. You can't make it happen all by yourself and, if you feel this is what's happening, it's not right. The relationships you focus on should be mutually supportive, caring, and nurturing.

Life Lesson Stop giving more to people who haven't rewarded or responded to your investment in them so far, and start giving your precious focus to those who do.

A Challenge Make a deal with yourself to focus your energies on people whose behavior shows that you matter to them. Promise yourself you'll stop trying to impress those with whom it's always a one-way street (you know who they are).

Do This Do the rounds of the people you love and like best. Ask someone out whom you fancy! Arrange a date night.

Don't Do This Ignore the red flags of disinterest, disdain, or disapproval in a relationship you've wanted to make work.

Who? Water signs (Pisces, Cancer, and Scorpio). People who love you and are worthy of your love too.

When? Up to a two-day time span. Summer. Possibly March, July, or November.

Is This a Yes or a No? Yes. Follow your heart.

THREE OF CUPS

Advice for Right Now/Today We're here for a good time, not a long time. Life is a journey to be experienced fully, enjoyed wholly, and lived as largely and as well as possible. Make the most of everything available to you today and savor all the potential for joy, connection, and growth that you encounter. You are wealthy in time, energy, and possibility. Don't waste any of it. Live your precious life to the full!

Affirmation I light up the room.

A Reassurance You are absolutely entitled to and permitted to have fun, live well, and enjoy your life. We are only here once. Make the most of it.

Life Lesson Life is infinitely better lived with the attitude of "everything's going to be alright." That's because, most of the time, it is. And when it isn't, well, you can focus on handling the hardships as they come. Don't waste your day living in dread or fear of what might (never) happen.

A Challenge Be a bearer of joy today. See yourself as the person who lights up the room, who brightens the mood, who lifts others up, and who creates magic and positivity where there is dullness or fear. Fake it till you make it! Today is going to be special.

Do This Socialize. Be kind to someone in need. Deliberately plan and do something to make someone else's day special. Be grateful for all your gifts. See the good in life.

Don't Do This Focus on the negative. Overthink the worst possible outcomes. Dwell on regrets.

Who? Water signs (Pisces, Cancer, and Scorpio). People who are a good time and bring you much laughter and happiness.

When? Up to a three-day time span. Summer. Possibly March, July, or November.

Is This a Yes or a No? Yes. It will be fun.

FOUR OF CUPS

Advice for Right Now/Today Refocus on what is right under your nose and has perhaps been missing out on your attention, gratitude, care, or action today. We often coast along, taking for granted what has always been there, supported us, or had our back. It's easy to stop noticing the constants. And it's easy then to start thinking that we're lacking in material things or that others have it better. Don't fall deeper into this trap today. Consciously stop the drift. Notice what you've got. Appreciate it.

Affirmation I am grateful for my blessings and for the life I'm living.

A Reassurance It's never too late to show gratitude, to express your appreciation, or to refocus your attention. It's the act of a moment, and it can wipe out weeks and months of inattention if performed sincerely and from the heart. It's never too late.

Life Lesson The grass is never automatically greener elsewhere. The grass is greenest where it's best looked after.

A Challenge Practicing gratitude increases self-awareness. When you notice what you rely on, what you need, and what you expect and when you see the things that form your bedrock, foundation, or safety net, you'll know where your sense of security resides. Otherwise, you might learn the hard way—you won't know what you've got (and need) till it's gone.

Do This Make a gratitude list. Call up or write to people you care about and owe appreciation to. Play to a strength. Build on a success. Revisit a role or place that made you happy.

Don't Do This Think that everything will be better by your escaping or starting something new.

Who? Water signs (Pisces, Cancer, and Scorpio). People who deserve more attention from you.

When? Up to a four-day time span. Summer. Possibly March, July, or November.

Is This a Yes or a No? Yes, if it involves something you already have.

FIVE OF CUPS

Advice for Right Now/Today Today, an emotional echo may bubble up for you from a loss or grief-provoking event in the past. Loss is always very hard for humans. We are hardwired to resist it on every level. And an ending, like the ending of any story, can shift our perception of what preceded it. That is the level on which you should engage with this emotion today. Let it teach or show you something new about your past and your story.

Affirmation I allow myself to feel these emotions and let go.

A Reassurance We all experience loss; it's inevitable, unavoidable, and part of what it means to live a long life. Remember that this too shall pass. Remember that nothing lasts forever. Be glad you had what you had and trust that there is more in store for you ahead.

Life Lesson You can't skip grief. Your body and mind both need to process your loss, and each has its own timetable and methods of doing so, some of which will remain a mystery to even you. Life can only be understood backward, but it must be lived forward. It's a balance to look back and understand but also to focus on and prioritize what's ahead.

A Challenge Don't dive into your emotional echo chamber, reliving the pain and picking at the wound. Strive to revisit the event from a safe distance, put things into perspective, reshape your personal narrative, and seek the wisdom that comes from understanding.

Do This Grieve. Cry. Release pent-up emotion. Journal. Talk it out. Do yoga (focusing on your hips, shoulders, and neck, where we store a lot of emotion). Get a massage. Reminisce about the good times.

Don't Do This Dwell on the pain and loss. Relive the trauma.

Who? Water signs (Pisces, Cancer, and Scorpio). People who are compassionate, caring, and available to listen to you today.

When? Up to a five-day time span. Summer. Possibly March, July, or November.

Is This a Yes or a No? No. This might be a step backwards.

SIX OF CUPS

Advice for Right Now/Today A joyful day is ahead. It will be filled with affection, play, and nostalgia. It's possible that something, someplace, or someone from your past (that you once held enormous affection for) is going to make a comeback—a welcome one. Maybe you should even consider reuniting with something lost yourself. The past could yield a surprising key to your future happiness.

Affirmation I am attracting joy, love, and playfulness from the past and present.

A Reassurance Our default factory settings lead us toward seeking (elusive) happiness and, for many, this takes the form of living in the past—the golden days or the era of safety and carefree freedom. But the past is not a glowing, joyful utopia. It was as fraught then as our present is now; we just gloss over and forget those parts. Don't ever think your best days are behind you. But also don't close the door to things, places, activities, or people from your past that could still serve a new role in your future.

Life Lesson Anything can be repurposed, reinvented, redesigned, and recalibrated to suit what's going on or needed now, and that includes your own past endeavors. Keep the door ajar to your past and you'll always have options.

A Challenge Walk down Memory Lane in your mind's eye and notice where your attention focuses. Notice where you feel nostalgia, regret, joy, and longing. Identify the people, places, activities, or roles you actually miss and would like to rekindle. Today's the day.

Do This Extend an olive branch. Visit old haunts. Get out your old photos. Organize a reunion.

Don't Do This Overemphasize the happiness you felt in your past and believe that was your peak.

Who? Water signs (Pisces, Cancer, and Scorpio). People you still think about, miss, and would like to reconnect with.

When? Up to a six-day time span. Summer. Possibly March, July, or November.

Is This a Yes or a No? Yes. You know you truly want this.

SEVEN OF CUPS

Advice for Right Now/Today Have faith in your ideas, fantasies, visions, and ideals today. What resides in your imagination is uniquely your own, and it's up to you what you do with it. You may think your daydreams are just play or frivolity, but what if they're actually divine guidance or personalized blueprints showing you how your life could (or should) be lived? If you don't act on what you think or feel, you'll never know if it could have been amazing. Take your daydreams seriously today.

Affirmation My imagination powers me.

A Reassurance Albert Einstein believed imagination was more important than knowledge because knowledge is limited to what we know now, whereas imagination is limitless and eternal. Release yourself to your imagination and trust that these daydreams visit you for a reason.

Life Lesson Vision without execution is just a daydream. Execution without vision is just keeping yourself busy and passing time. You have to learn to marry your vision with your actions to fulfill your true potential in life.

A Challenge Invest time and effort in connecting with, clarifying, describing, and researching your wildest fantasies and daydreams. Get them on paper. Prioritize what you can work on.

Do This Make a mood board. Brainstorm. Meditate. Doodle. Talk to the mirror about your ideal self, lifestyle, home, work, and purpose.

Don't Do This Ignore the ideas, themes, realities, and desires that play on your mind.

Who? Water signs (Pisces, Cancer, and Scorpio). People who are creative, inspired, enlightened, and eager to help you realize your dreams.

When? Up to a seven-day time span. Summer. Possibly March, July, or November.

Is This a Yes or a No? Yes. Live the dream.

EIGHT OF CUPS

Advice for Right Now/Today Stop banging your head against a brick wall. Stop forcing or pushing something that is simply not working for you. Today, release things that aren't working, be they roles, relationships, goals, tasks, projects, or chores. I promise that better opportunities lie ahead, but they can't emerge and enter your life unless there's room. So have a clearout and be ready to walk away.

Affirmation If the door won't open, it's not my door.

A Reassurance It takes great courage to accept something isn't working and be proactive about withdrawing from it. It's not quitting, nor is it failure. It's being realistic, honest, and protective of your own precious time and energy.

Life Lesson Disappointment is the herald of wisdom. Success often follows a failure. You live and learn and go again.

A Challenge Be totally honest about where you're making sacrifices but not getting results. Where are you feeling consistent resistance, lack, or emptiness? Is this still worth it? Do you have another viable plan? Be honest. Ask for feedback if you find it hard to be objective.

Do This Embrace honest assessment. List your sacrifices and whether they have led to rewards. Notice where your efforts are one-sided.

Don't Do This Make excuses for people or situations that aren't benefiting you despite your best efforts.

Who? Water signs (Pisces, Cancer, and Scorpio). People who are maybe not as invested in you as you are in them.

When? Up to an eight-day time span. Summer. Possibly March, July, or November.

Is This a Yes or a No? No. Move on to something better.

NINE OF CUPS

Advice for Right Now/Today We've got big dream-come-true energy with this card! Today is going to be great, with the potential to be magical, lucky, surprising, and successful. You can go further than you thought possible and do whatever you dream of. The important thing is to be open and confident. If you want that promotion, ask for it. Lay out your case and be proactive; shade or game-playing will only muddy the waters. Head in a straight line toward what you most want.

Affirmation I am ready for my wildest dreams to come true.

A Reassurance Dreams don't work unless you take action. The surest way to make your dreams come true is to live them. Today is the first day of new life. Enjoy it.

Life Lesson The only limit you put on yourself is the limit of your dreams and imagination.

A Challenge Know your desires. Clarify your goals. Express your ideals. And fake it till you make it! Act like these things are already manifesting for you. Do what you'd do if this were all happening, and you will accelerate the opportunities.

Do This Write down your dearest wish and pray for it to happen. Take an action that helps get you closer. Believe in yourself. Be positive. Be bold.

Don't Do This Sit and wait and hope for something to happen to you. Make it happen.

Who? Water signs (Pisces, Cancer, and Scorpio). People who are part of your wish-come-true story—maybe the object of it or supporters of it.

When? Up to a nine-day time span. Summer. Possibly March, July, or November.

Is This a Yes or a No? Yes. Pursue your dreams.

TEN OF CUPS

Advice for Right Now/Today Relationship bliss. Emotional fulfillment. Feeling loved, needed, supported, and rewarded. This is what today has in store, so draw closer to the people you think this applies to and revel in the beautiful bonds and chemistry you enjoy with them. Celebrate your best people. Let yourself fall in love. Promise it's forever. Build exciting plans with those you trust. Actively design your future together.

Affirmation I want to make magical plans for the future with people I love.

A Reassurance Feeling loved makes you feel strong and supported, and loving someone makes you feel brave and needed. Never underestimate the power of these feelings—they keep you young, healthy, and happy. Celebrate, nurture, and appreciate your favorite people today.

Life Lesson Relationships aren't about the destination; they're about the journey. And those journeys should be fun and enjoyable. It doesn't happen by itself, so put some time and effort into making your relationship journeys magical and joyful.

A Challenge What future plans can you dream up, research, and organize with the people you love and like? Make an investment in your shared goals, dreams, and ideals. Bring the energy and ideas.

Do This Socialize. Treat the people you love. Book outings, trips, and events. Tell them how you feel and how much you appreciate them. Propose.

Don't Do This Feel alone instead of focusing on the people in your life who are positive influences and love you.

Who? Water signs (Pisces, Cancer, and Scorpio). People you love.

When? Up to a ten-day time span. Summer. Possibly March, July, or November.

Is This a Yes or a No? Yes. Joy lies ahead with this route.

Conclusion

I hope this book has helped to breathe new life into your tarot deck (or decks, if you're like me). Tarot is useful, helpful, wise, and decisive. It is an ally in this strange, scary, overwhelming, ever-changing world we live in and must make the best of.

I want everyone to feel confident and at ease with their deck. And I figured the easiest way for that to start to happen (no matter where you take it from here) was to reduce it to its most basic elements by focusing on one-card pulls.

You can answer your question with one card! You can and you will. In fact, it will sharpen your questioning skills (and we all know that if you ask the right question, you're halfway there) and start to wake up your intuition, your subconscious, and your reflective powers.

Try and pull a card every day, for one reason or another. Bring your tarot cards into your daily life and let them guide you through the ups, downs, and crossroads. Your deck contains at least 500 years' worth of human wisdom and experience, and that has to mean something. Nothing we're facing is new. Everything's been done, felt, seen, and endured before.

I wish you truthful, comforting, and hopeful readings. I wish you well.

Acknowledgments

Thank you to Quarto for being superduper to work with (especially Hilary, Anne, and Lydia). This is our second book together, and it's been a real pleasure.

Thank you to Adam Oehlers for illustrating this book to a level beyond my wildest dreams and making it the enchanting guide I wished for. I am humbly grateful for your talented contribution.

Thank you, as always and ever, to my allies on the "other side." I know you are helping me, I appreciate your guidance and love, and I can't wait to see you all again one day, albeit hopefully not too soon. There's life to be lived yet!

Thank you to my wonderful family. We are a small but happy unit—Mum, Vicki, Debra, Alan, Will, Hannah, Freddie, and Alice.

And, of course, thank you to my steadfast, strong, and loving partner, Luke. You make all that I do and enjoy possible.

About the Author

KERRY WARD, a.k.a. Tarotbella, has been reading and teaching tarot cards for more than twenty-five years, utilizing a blend of tarot, astrology, and numerology to deliver personal readings for clients all over the globe. She writes for many titles worldwide and is the author of *Power, Purpose, Practice* and the creator of *The Good Karma Tarot* and co-creator of *The Crystal Magic Tarot*. She lives in Nottingham, England with her partner, Luke, and their cats, Willow, Peaches, and Tron.

About the Illustrator

ADAM OEHLERS (ADAM OEHLERS ILLUSTRATION) is an illustrator currently working out of Norwich, England.

He has exhibited worldwide from Australia, to the UK, Europe, and the States. He has worked alongside writers and publishers from around the world, as well as concept artists, character designers, and writers for animations. He has also worked as a set dressing artist for film and television. He has worked on many tarot decks as well as the award winning "Oak, Ash and Thorn" with Three Trees Tarot, which was his introduction into the world of tarot.

Adam has always found a great deal of inspiration from the classic illustrations of Arthur Rackham, Edward Gorey, and any intricate classic pen illustrations and print work. He has a great love of old stories and fairy tales and aims to tell a story through every illustration. In his work, he strives to create a sense of nostalgia to take the viewer back to a forgotten memory, with the goal of reminding them of the soft magic that surrounds us.

www.adamoehlersillustration.com | Instagram @adamoehlers

Index